How to Write A Philosophy Paper

James S. Stramel
Santa Monica College

University Press of America, Inc.
Lanham • New York • London

Copyright © 1995 by
James S. Stramel
University Press of America,® Inc.
4720 Boston Way
Lanham, Maryland 20706

3 Henrietta Street
London, WC2E 8LU England

Library of Congress Cataloging-in-Publication Data
Stramel, James S. (James Sidney)
How to write a philosophy paper / James S. Stramel
p.   cm.
Includes bibliographical references and index
1. Philosophy – Study and teaching (Higher)   2. Written
Communication. I. Title.
B52.S84   1994
808' . 0661–dc20   94-38264 CIP

ISBN 0-8191-9778-5 (pbk.: alk paper)

Dedicated to the memory of Professor Irwin "Chet" Lieb,
who taught me how to teach,

and to philosophy students everywhere.

Contents

Preface

Some students beginning the study of philosophy find it easy, while many others find it very difficult. Almost all of them find it strange. I cannot count the number of times students have told me that they "have never done anything like this before." This is both surprising and perfectly expectable. It is surprising because philosophy requires careful and rigorous thinking in the construction and evaluation of arguments, and this—one hopes—is something that students encounter in all fields of study. On the other hand, it is not surprising at all since students in introductory philosophy classes are confronted with issues and problems that they are unlikely to have explored elsewhere in the manner characteristic of philosophers. As one of my senior undergraduate students said about the essay he was struggling with, "I've never had to *think* before!" This remark is telling in that the kind of writing expected of students in most other classes usually does not call on them to use and develop their skills of conceptual analysis and argumentation.

Most introductory courses in philosophy require that students do some writing, usually short essays or term papers. But rarely do these courses provide students with any substantive guidance as to *how to write a philosophical essay*. The instructor may make a few suggestions in addition to specifying the paper's requirements, but when it comes down to the actual work of thinking and writing, most students find themselves adrift. Thus, the assignment of writing a philosophy paper can provoke the sort of response illustrated on the cover.

There are, of course, numerous "Introductions to Philosophy" which discuss the 'ins and outs' of philosophical practice, but few of these offer specific advice on the composing of essays. Even if students are made aware of this kind of literature, they usually find it too voluminous to digest in time to actually *write* their essay. Others will not make the effort to consult this literature, hoping to somehow muddle through. Still others will simply procrastinate beyond the point of redemption.

What the beginning student of philosophy needs is a short, "user friendly" guide to writing philosophical essays that: is manageable in length and content; provides a ready arsenal of analytical and compositional techniques; and is inexpensive enough to satisfy the most cost-conscious students and instructors. The purpose of this handbook is to reduce the anxiety, and increase the rewards, that come from writing thoughtful philosophical essays.

How to Use this Handbook

This booklet can be read in a few hours. My hope (and suggestion) is that students read it very early in their course, so that all their philosophical efforts may benefit. Then, when it comes time to write, the student will already be acquainted with the principles of good philosophical thinking and writing.

Since good philosophical writing is, for the most part, just good philosophical thinking *on paper*, much of this handbook presents and explains the most important concepts and tools needed for sound philosophical thinking. Some of these tools may be discussed by your professor, or you may have studied the principles of reasoning in a logic or critical thinking class. I have provided these materials for those students who may not otherwise be familiar with them, or who may benefit from a "refresher course."

How to Write a Philosophy Paper is organized to lead you from the very first stages of philosophical reflection to the final draft of your paper. The most effective way to use it is to read from beginning to end long before you start writing. However, you may simply refer to the various sections as you need them in the process of writing. In any case, I strongly recommend that you take the time to read all the sections. It would *not* be a good idea to simply skip to Chapter V on Composition. Chapters I - IV discuss important features that are characteristic of *philosophical writing* as opposed to other types of writing.

Chapter 1

The Enterprise of Philosophy

There are almost as many descriptions of what philosophy is as there are philosophers. Because philosophical inquiry is so multi-faceted, it is difficult to give a definition of it that will satisfy all philosophers. Nevertheless, everyone agrees that philosophy as a practice is an activity of reason directed at fundamentally important matters of all kinds.

The Greek word "philosophy" literally means "the love of wisdom." The goal of philosophical inquiry, then, is to achieve understanding and wisdom of the broadest and deepest kind. In this search for wisdom, the philosopher is guided by a passion for truth, employing careful reasoning in the continuous examination of our beliefs and basic assumptions. We strive toward rationality, away from emotion, authority, and tradition. This impartial search for truth requires tolerance and openness to a wide spectrum of ideas, even ones which contradict one's intuitions or firmly held beliefs. Philosophical inquiry is marked by the compelling obligation to give *reasons* for whatever we affirm or conclude. Any view or claim, no matter how outrageous, may be introduced for discussion, provided only that its proponent endeavors adequately to support it by argument. It is not enough to disagree or even to point out that some claim is false. Philosophical criticism often begins with disagreement, but it does not end there. Philosophical criticism is *reasoned* disagreement, and there is an argument to be dealt with.

1

Philosophers are characterized by an inquiring and reflective attitude. This insatiable intellectual curiosity leads to
* the analysis and definition of key concepts,
* the identification of basic beliefs and assumptions,
* the comparison, criticism, and evaluation of alternative positions,
* the gathering of evidence and the construction of arguments,
* the careful consideration of criticisms and objections.

Socrates held that the goal of philosophical inquiry is not to answer questions, but to question answers. Purported answers must be carefully analyzed for clarity and reasonableness, rigorously compared to alternative proposals, and evaluated for their overall adequacy.

Philosophy is both a way of thinking about the world and a way of thinking *about our thinking.* In this regard, philosophy is the study of the rational, cognitive, or conceptual activities of persons. As such, it is better thought of as a method rather than as a subject matter. Accordingly, there is the "philosophy of" almost anything: philosophy of science, philosophy of religion, of art, of law, even the philosophy of sex and love! Philosophy is thus a "second order" discipline, one step removed from the practice of the scientist, theologian, or artist. It is not an inquiry into the "first order" facts, but into the methods by which we search for such facts, the grounds or reasons on the basis of which we assert them, and the concepts we use in formulating them.

For example, the historian typically attempts to learn what events took place at some time and place in the past, what events were the causes of later events, etc. By contrast, the philosopher of history will be led to ask about *the concept of history* itself: What is historical knowledge? What is "the past"? Is it real? "Real" in what sense? How does the past relate to or affect the present?, the future? Is it possible for historians to discover the truth about the past, or is history only a subjective and distorted interpretation of the evidence we now have of past events? These are philosophical—not historical—questions.

History, science, theology, art, mathematics, education, music, and all other fields are grounded in particular assumptions about reality, values, and appropriate methodologies. Persons who work in these fields typically work only on the "first-order" questions, and do not question the foundations—the basic principles—of their discipline in this way. This task is usually taken up by the philosopher. (Of course, a few practitioners of these disciplines still sometimes *also* wear the philosopher's cap.)

It is often said that philosophy begins in wonder. We have all entertained questions like the following at one time or another: "Where did the world come from?" "How do we know what's right and what's wrong?" "What happens to me when I die?" "Does the light really go out when you close the refrigerator door?" Of course, only the first three of these questions are philosophical; the last is a parody of "philosophical" curiosity. But even a humorous and half-serious question like the one about the refrigerator light can quickly lead us into the realm of philosophy. We probably have some confidence that the light *does go out*; but what is the source of that confidence? After all, has anyone ever crawled inside a refrigerator to verify this? But *now* we must ask whether we can know only those things we can experience first-hand. Or, can we claim to know things on the basis of authority? These are philosophical questions about the nature and extent of human knowledge.

This kind of persistent search for deeper, more fundamental answers may remind you of the precocious child who asks, "Why is such-and-such?"; and when told again asks, "But why is *that*?" and so on incessantly, until we suggest that (s)he go play outside! Philosophers are a little bit like young children—always probing for deeper answers. Philosophy starts with questions and seeks answers, though one does not fail to do philosophy—even do it well—if one does not reach an acceptable answer. Consequently, much time is spent on the careful formulation of significant questions. Like so many human activities, much of the pleasure of doing philosophy lies in the activity itself.

Some questions are philosophical, but many are not. How are we to distinguish the two? The distinction between philosophical and non-philosophical inquiry is difficult to make precise, but it can be illustrated by distinguishing between three general types of questions that might interest us with respect to a given topic. Suppose, for example, you are interested in the American penal system. Many of our prisons are already overcrowded, so a pressing concern is whether we will have enough space for convicted offenders. This is a purely *factual* question, one which could be answered by gathering sufficient information about projected crime rates, sentencing policies, and prison capacity. In thinking about this issue, you might also wonder whether the government should build a new large-capacity prison. This is a *value* question, one whose answer depends on the needs and desires (the 'values') of society. These two questions may obviously be related: if you learn that we desperately need prison space, then you may think that we should have a new prison. Of course, this need must be balanced against numerous other considerations: availability of funds and a suitable location, the appropriateness of current sentencing policies, etc.

Although factual and value questions can be difficult to answer, they are not *philosophical* questions. However, the pursuit of any subject will inevitably lead one to confront philosophical problems. To continue with our example, you might be led to wonder whether imprisonment is a just form of punishment. In raising this issue you are asking a *conceptual question*: in order to answer, you must ask what the concept of justice allows or requires for the treatment of individuals in relation to society. In short, you must ask, "What is justice?" Then you must determine whether imprisonment satisfies the conditions which define the concept of justice. These are matters that can be settled only by thinking philosophically about them.

Here are a few more examples of non-philosophical questions that give rise to philosophical questions:

Non-philosophical: "Am I a good person?"
Philosophical: "What does it mean to be a good person?" "What is moral virtue?" "What is the virtuous life?"

Non-philosophical: "How do scientists measure time?"
Philosophical: "What is Time?" "Is time-travel possible?"

Non-philosophical: "How do glasses correct visual problems?"
Philosophical: "Do we see things as they really are 'in themselves'?" "Is color an objective property of objects, or does its perception depend on the way our eyes and brains are constructed?"

Philosophical questions, then, are not just challenging questions, but challenging questions of a particular sort. They are the deep, conceptual questions that go beyond, or get behind, factual or value questions.

This point has an important moral for writing your philosophy paper: *a philosophical question cannot be answered solely by an appeal to factual or value-based data.* It can only be answered by determining what the correct analysis of the central concepts are, and whether a particular thing, person, or action satisfies the conditions set by that analysis.

Aristotle asserted that "all men by nature desire to know." For many of us, the desire to find answers to the important questions is inescapable. If we are curious and reflective, we cannot avoid confronting the important philosophical issues associated with virtually every aspect of our lives. We philosophize whenever we give reasons for any sort of stance or position—whenever we present or examine arguments for claims that something is true or real.

Philosophy is pursued by intelligent beings who want to understand themselves and their world—it is not the sole province of the professional philosopher. The difference between philosophers and ordinary people is one of degree and not kind. The philosopher attempts to make his or her philosophical stance explicit and to express and defend it in clear language. Through the careful structuring of arguments, the goal is organization and synthesis, systematization and consistency. This is something that we all do, whether we think of ourselves as doing philosophy or not. The formal study of philosophy encourages us to do it in a careful, reasonable way. It invites us to think more rigorously, intentionally, seriously and thoroughly.

Philosophical thinking helps us to clarify issues and stances, to discriminate between options, and make better decisions. Due to the connection between belief and action, philosophy can help us to lead better lives. Because philosophical questions emerge from reflection about ourselves and our relations to others and the world, and because our lives are complex and ever-changing, there will always be new questions to investigate. It should not dismay you to learn that there is no end to philosophical inquiry. It can be a fascinating and exciting path to personal fulfillment, helping us to achieve a greater awareness of ourselves, our world, and our place in it.

A. *Approaches To Philosophical Writing*

Philosophical writing can take many forms. The most common, of course, is the essay, but good philosophy has also appeared in the form of dialogue, drama, fiction and even poetry. We will focus on the essay form for a number of reasons. First, this is most likely the form that will be assigned by your instructor; second, it is the easiest to handle in the classroom; and third, it is the standard form in philosophy. Students who are particularly creative (or anxious to seem so to their instructor) may be tempted to try their hand at dialogue. For the novice this is almost always a bad idea. Despite appearances, the dialogue is a difficult form to master and it offers numerous dangers. Two of these are: the ease with which one can stray from the issues; and the tendency toward cuteness at the expense of philosophical rigor.

There are two main approaches to the study of philosophy—*historical* and *critical*—and these may be reflected in the type of essay you will be asked to write. The historical approach concentrates on the contributions of acknowledged philosophers. The critical approach stresses involvement in the activity of philosophizing, building a personal philosophy of life, asking questions and seeking answers that make a personal difference, identifying and clarifying assumptions, making distinctions and seeking out new perspectives. By examining the views of other philosophers students are forced to speculate about the range of possibilities and this can help them to find their own positions.

We can divide philosophical essays roughly into two types: the *expository* and the *argumentative*. It is probably best to see them as occupying opposite ends of a continuum as they are not mutually exclusive, and almost any philosophical essay will contain elements of both.

You are probably already familiar with writing expository essays from other courses. Here the emphasis is on showing that you are familiar with and understand the details of X's theory of such-and-such. For example, you might be asked to write an expository essay on Aristotle's theory of moral virtue. In its purest form, the expository essay is little more than a "book report," requiring only the ability to accurately paraphrase what someone else has written. There is nothing particularly challenging, and certainly almost nothing philosophically interesting, about such a task. Students are not likely to be engaged by the project and instructors are certain to be bored reading the results. Even an assignment which asks you to "compare and contrast" (say, Hume's and Kant's ethical theories) is little better. Such assignments do not invite the student to engage in the practice of doing philosophy.

We hope (and recommend) that students will be invited to accept the challenge of *doing* philosophy by addressing a philosophical question or problem in an argumentative essay. This is certainly more difficult than mere exposition, but it is far more rewarding.

Of course, most students can't just jump in cold and start constructing elaborate and ingenious theories. One of the best ways to learn about philosophy is to start reading the works of philosophers, to see what kinds of problems engaged them, and to see how they go about finding solutions. Most courses will have you read selections from a small number of history's greatest philosophers, and the instructor will lecture on the material. Usually a variety of philosophical problems will be introduced and explored to varying degrees. Almost any of these could yield a suitable and manageable topic for your essay.

Chapter 2

Thinking Philosophically

One main goal of philosophical inquiry is to come to a reasoned position on a topic and state clearly what you believe to be true. This requires a science of communication: we must choose and define terms carefully, relate concepts systematically, and organize experience and ideas into intelligible prose. The test of one's comprehension is the extent to which one can express ideas or thoughts in a logical and intelligible manner.

It has been said that "half of good philosophy is good grammar." Ungrammatical language and tortured sentences are often sure signs of unclear or confused thinking. If your writing is grammatically out of control you are probably trying to express a thought you don't yet have under control.

So good philosophical writing is grammatical. But it would be a *fallacy* (a bit of faulty reasoning) to infer that all grammatical writing is therefore good philosophical writing. Of course, much more must be said about composition, but we shouldn't get the cart before the horse. The point of good writing is to effectively convey your *ideas* on your topic. So we should first spend some time discussing good philosophical thinking.

A. *Argumentation*

The real work in philosophy gets done in arguments, so if your paper is devoid of arguments it is not really a philosophy paper. As a first approximation, an *argument* is the presentation of reasons for believing a given claim. Some reasons are more convincing than others, so arguments can range in strength from very compelling to utterly worthless. Perhaps the most important task in philosophical writing is the arrangement of claims into arguments; hence the logical relations of claims to one another become crucial. Critical thinking is usually judged by the extent to which arguments are organized and presented in a systematic way.

Before we dig in, notice that the philosophically relevant sense of "argument" must be distinguished from a quarrel. People often have arguments in this latter sense, but that doesn't mean they're doing philosophy (though they might be). Here is the definition of "argument":

> *An ARGUMENT is a set of two or more claims (statements or assertions) all but one of which are called the "premises," and the other is called the "conclusion," where the premises are intended to logically support the conclusion.*

Notice that the definition does not say that the premises *do* support the conclusion—that would make every argument a *good* argument, by definition. But there are certainly plenty of bad arguments floating around. What it means for premises to 'logically support' a conclusion will be addressed shortly. The figure below shows the general, schematic form for all arguments.

```
1. Premise
2. Premise
   .       .
   .       .
   .       .
n. Premise
_____
n+1. Conclusion
```

In the illustration "n" is a variable representing the number of premises in the argument. So if an argument has five premises, the conclusion will be numbered "6." The simplest arguments have only one premise, although most of the arguments you are likely to encounter will have at least two. Arguments much longer than this are possible, though these can usually be seen as complex arguments made up of simpler arguments linked together.

Here is an example of an argument that might be offered against abortion:

1. Taking an innocent life except to save a life is wrong.
2. Abortion is the taking of an innocent life.
3. Therefore, abortion is wrong except to save a life.

The first two claims (the premises) are offered as reasons to believe the third (the conclusion), so we have an argument. How to determine whether the argument is any good will be addressed shortly.

Arguments have traditionally been divided into two general types: *deductive* and *inductive*. Most of the arguments you are likely to encounter and use in a philosophy course will be deductive. In the next few sections we shall concentrate on deductive arguments: their nature; how to identify and evaluate them; how to construct them; and how to avoid some common forms of fallacious reasoning.

1. *Argument Identification*

Before you can evaluate an argument you must know what the argument is. If it is an argument that *you* are trying to construct this should not be too difficult. If it is an argument that is found in the work of an author you have read, this can be more difficult. Most authors do not explicitly lay out their arguments for you in standard argument form (see preceding box), so you will usually have to do a bit of work to isolate the actual premises and conclusion from the text. Very often, the author will give you some "linguistic signposts" in the form of premise- and conclusion-indicators. Words like "since," "because," and "for" will usually be followed by a premise. Claims *preceded* by the expressions "... implies that," "... shows that," and "... establishes that" are also premises. Words like "therefore," "hence," "consequently," "so," and "thus" will be followed by the conclusion.

A word of warning: when we reconstruct an argument in standard form the conclusion always appears last, but spoken and written arguments are not bound by this rule. Sometimes the conclusion is presented first, or it can appear between two premises. Premises may appear in any order; and remarks that are not actually part of the argument may be thrown in at any point. This is why identifying an argument is sometimes difficult.

Here is a short passage containing an argument. See if you can pick out the premises and the conclusion. (For ease of reference we have numbered the claims consecutively.)

(1) The idea of a free press in America today is a joke. (2) A small group of people, the nation's advertisers, control the media more effectively than if they owned it outright. (3) Through fear of an advertising boycott they can dictate everything from programming to news report content. (4) Politicians as well as editors shiver in their boots at the thought of such a boycott. (5) This situation is intolerable and ought to be changed.

It is usually best to locate the conclusion first, which is easy if there is a conclusion-indicator present.   Unfortunately, this passage contains no conclusion-indicators, so we have to ask what point the author is trying to establish by giving supporting reasons (of course, it is *always* a good idea to do this). Actually, there seem to be *two* claims that could be seen as the conclusion of the argument: the first and the last sentences. To decide which is the conclusion it is helpful to look at the other claims to see if they function as reasons for believing one or the other of our potential conclusions. In this case it is clear that claims 2-4 support claim 1: they are reasons for thinking that the American press is not really free. Claim 5 expresses a value judgment about the state of the press, and includes a call to action.

Notice, too, that claims 2, 3, and 4 are not all on a par: claims 3 and 4 are reasons to believe that advertisers control the media (2), and this claim, in turn, directly supports the main conclusion, (1). We *could* represent these claims as comprising two *separate* arguments, but it would be better to say that we have one slightly complicated argument where some premises lead to an intermediate conclusion which, in turn, supports the main conclusion. This is an important and useful feature of argumentation: the conclusion of one argument can often be used as a premise in a new argument, thus creating a chain of ideas.

Retaining the numbering above, here is the argument in standard form:

1. (3) Advertisers, through fear of a boycott, can dictate programming.
2. (4) Politicians and editors shiver at the thought of a boycott.
3. (2) (Therefore) The nation's advertisers control the media.
4. (1) *Therefore*, the idea of a free press in America is a joke.

The author *may* take this argument to provide some reason to believe 5, in which case 5 would be listed as yet another (further) conclusion of the argument. It is not always clear whether an author *intends* some claims to logically support others.

2. *Argument Evaluation*

Once an argument is set out before you, you must decide whether it is a *good* argument. That is, you must determine whether you should accept the conclusion on the basis of the premises. We often have an intuitive sense of whether an argument is good or bad, but sometimes not, especially if the argument is long or complicated. We need to get more precise. Arguments can be evaluated with respect to their *form* or their *content*.

a. *Deductive Validity: The First Criterion*

The evaluation of an argument with respect to its form or structure concerns its *validity*. The premises of a good deductive argument provide *conclusive* logical support for the conclusion. This relation of "logical support" is cashed out in terms of the concept of *validity*:

An argument is VALID if and only if it is not possible for all the premises to be true and the conclusion to be false (simultaneously).

Deductively valid arguments are "truth-preserving," in the sense that *if* the premises are true then the conclusion *must* be true as well. The premises of a valid argument *entail* the conclusion.

Here is an example of a valid argument: an argument that is "good" in virtue of its form:

1. If Michael Jackson is a bullfrog, then he has four legs.
2. Michael is a bullfrog.
3. Therefore, Michael has four legs.

If it seems to you that there is something wrong with this argument, you're right; we'll get to that in a moment. We didn't say the argument was flawless, only that it is *valid*. By using capital letters to represent the individual claims that appear in the argument we can express its form like this:

1. If P, then Q.
2. P.
3. Therefore, Q.

No matter what claims we put in for P and Q (no matter what the content) the resulting argument will be valid: *if* the premises are true then the conclusion must be true as well. This is why validity is a purely structural or formal property of arguments.

To determine whether an argument is valid or not, *suppose* that all the premises are true (whether they really are or not) and ask if, on that assumption, it is possible for the conclusion to be false. If not, then the argument is valid; if so, then it is invalid. (If this isn't clear to you yet, refer back to the definition of validity, and try again.)

Here is another example of a valid argument:

1. Either the moon is made of green cheese or Elvis is alive and working in a gas station on 7th Street.
2. As everyone knows, the moon is *not* made of green cheese.
3. Therefore, Elvis is alive and working in a gas station on 7th Street.

If the premises of this argument were true, then the conclusion would have to be true as well, so the argument is valid. If it is true that *either* M or E is the case, and we know M is not the case, then E must be the case.

Notice that it follows from the definition of validity that it is possible for there to be valid arguments that in fact have false premises and a true conclusion, or even false premises and a false conclusion. The only combination that validity rules out is true premises supporting a false conclusion. Consider this example:

1. All blondes are dentists.
2. All dentists are Republicans.
3. Therefore, all blondes are Republicans.

The premises of this argument are both false and so is the conclusion. Still, the argument is valid. This may seem surprising, but remember that validity only ensures that *if* the premises are true, then the conclusion must be true too. Validity is truth-preserving, but it does not claim or ensure that the premises *are true*.

Here are some of the more common and useful valid argument forms (remember: "P" and "Q" here stand for complete claims):

Modus Ponens	**Modus Tollens**
(affirming the antecedent)[*]	(denying the consequent)[*]
If P, then Q	If P, then Q
P	Not Q
———————	———————
Q	Not P

Disjunctive Syllogism	**Hypothetical Syllogism**
Either P or Q	If P, then Q
Not P	If Q, then R
———————	———————
Q	If P, then R

[*]An 'If...then...' claim is called a *conditional*. The sub-claim following 'If' is the *antecedent* of the conditional; the sub-claim following 'then' is called the *consequent*.

There are also valid arguments that are obtained by substituting into certain argument forms expressions that are not complete sentences. Consider the following argument:

1. All right actions are actions that produce good consequences.
2. All actions that produce good consequences are actions that maximize happiness and minimize pain.
3. Therefore, all right actions are actions that maximize happiness and minimize pain.

This argument has the following (valid) form:

1. All X's are Y.
2. All Y's are Z.
   ———————
3. All X's are Z.

Here are three other common valid argument forms of this type (called categorical syllogisms because the claims relate members of categories or classes; a *syllogism* is a two-premise argument):

| No X's are Y. | All X's are Y. | All X's are Y. |
All Z's are X.	Some X's are Z.	Some X's are not Z.
No Z's are Y.	Some Y's are Z.	Some Y's are not Z.

b. Deductive Fallacies

As we have seen, there are a number of common and useful valid forms of reasoning. There are also a number of recognized *invalid* forms of reasoning (called fallacies) which are often mistaken for valid arguments. The most common error is mistaking an invalid argument for a valid one. Here are examples of a few of the most common deductive fallacies; symbolizations revealing the argument's form appear to the right:

1. If Smith voted in the last election, she must be a U.S. citizen.	1. If P, then Q.
2. In fact, Smith is a U.S. citizen.	2. Q
3. Therefore, Smith did vote in the last election.	3. P

It's true that only citizens can vote (premise 1), and let's suppose that Smith *is* a citizen (premise 2). Still, those two facts do not ensure that she voted—maybe she was out of the country on vacation. This invalid argument form is called *affirming the consequent.*

Here is another common invalid argument form, called *denying the antecedent:*

1. If John took a shower, then he got wet.	1. If P, then Q.
2. John didn't take a shower.	2. Not P.
3. Therefore, John didn't get wet.	3. Not Q.

Even if the premises were true the conclusion could still be false; maybe John got caught in the rain!

Here are two common *invalid* categorical syllogisms:

1. All men are humans.	1. All X's are Y's.
2. All women are humans.	2. All Z's are Y's.
3. Therefore, All men are women.	3. All X's are Z's.

1. All sophomores are undergraduates.	1. All X's are Y's.
2. No seniors are sophomores.	2. No Z's are X's.
3. Therefore, No undergraduates are seniors.	3. No Y's are Z's.

In the last two sections we have presented just some of the most common valid and invalid argument forms; for a more complete list and discussion of these forms consult any good Logic text (see the Bibliography).

c. *Modeling*

There are a number of occasions where you might want to show that a particular argument is invalid. You might, for example, be presented with an argument which you believe is fallacious. Or you might wish to bolster your own position by showing that an argument which seems to support the opposite conclusion is invalid.

One way to show that an argument is invalid is to construct an argument with the same form, but which everyone will agree proceeds from acceptable premises to an obviously unacceptable conclusion. This is the technique of Modeling. For example, in the *Meditations* Descartes argues from the premise "My senses sometimes deceive me" to the conclusion "It could be the case that my senses always deceive me." The form of this argument could be represented in this way:

1. X is sometimes F.
2. Therefore, it could be that X is always F.

All we need to do is find a pair of replacements for X and F that generate an obviously invalid argument. How about this?:

1. Paintings are sometimes forgeries.
2. Therefore, it could be that paintings are always forgeries.

The premise is clearly true, but the conclusion must be false. After all, a forged painting is a copy of some original painting, and it could not be the case that *all* paintings were copies. Notice, however, that we have shown only that any argument of this form is invalid; we haven't established that Descartes' conclusion is definitely false. He (or someone else) might have another argument that *is* successful in establishing that conclusion.

d. *Soundness: The Second Criterion*

While the arguments above about Michael Jackson and Elvis are valid, neither is a "good" argument in the complete sense that we should accept its conclusion as true on the basis of those premises. As you surely noticed, each argument relies on a false premise. This means that while the arguments are valid they are not also *sound*:

> *An argument is SOUND if and only if (1) the argument is Valid and (2) all its premises are in fact true.*

Soundness is validity plus true premises. To ask whether an argument is sound is to evaluate it with respect to its *content,* because we are now asking about the truth or falsity of the particular premises, and this is not a merely *formal* matter.

A "good" argument must be *both* valid and sound.

Here is a modification of the argument about Michael Jackson that is both valid and sound:

1. If Michael Jackson is a multi-millionaire, then he is rich.
2. Michael Jackson is a multi-millionaire.
3. Therefore, Michael Jackson is rich.

This argument has the same form as the original version (*modus ponens*), but now it also has true premises. So we can be sure that its conclusion is true.

A note about the proper use of these concepts: *validity* and *soundness* are properties of arguments—*not* of claims by themselves. With respect to claims, we are interested mainly in their truth or falsity. It makes no sense to speak of an argument being "true" *or* "false," or to speak of an individual claim being "valid" *or* "invalid," or "sound" *or* "unsound".

> In evaluating arguments:
> **first,** determine what the premises and conclusion are;
> **second,** check for Validity; and
> **third,** check for Soundness.

If an argument is either invalid or unsound then that argument does not compel our assent to the conclusion *on the basis of those premises*. Notice, however, that this does not rule out the possibility that there are *other* arguments which do!

Even if an argument is both valid and sound, it may still fail to compel the reader's assent, even though it should. This is probably because either the argument's structure is unclear, or the truth of the premises is obscured in some way, so the reader does not recognize that the argument is good. In other words, something about the way the argument is presented makes it hard to tell that it *is* both valid and sound. Remember that it is part of your task to make these things obvious to your reader. Explain the logical structure of your argument and provide the necessary evidence for its premises. The burden of proof is on you.

It is sometimes difficult to know just how much evidence is sufficient to convince the reader of the truth of your premises. Unless a premise is very obviously true, you should present some reasons (an argument!) for thinking it *is* true. But, what about the premises of *that* argument? Must you also argue for them? Obviously, you can't argue for everything, and this is not just because you don't have enough time or space! Some things will have to be accepted or assumed as basic (e.g., arithmetic and geometry are based on a set of axioms which are simply accepted as true). At some point you have to stop arguing for your premises. If you stop too early, your argument will rest on a controversial claim. If you stop too late, your argument becomes pedantic and wastes your and your reader's time.

Unfortunately, there is no neat formula for deciding what you must argue for and what you may assume. You obviously don't have to argue on behalf of established facts (whether scientific or otherwise). For any other claim, play devil's advocate: ask yourself whether you can think of any reasonable and significant objections to the claim. If so, then perhaps you should say something to remove any doubt.

In part, you will have to rely on common sense. But beware: things which seem obviously true to common sense are often discovered to be doubtful or even false when subjected to philosophical scrutiny. Common sense is everyone's starting point. Ordinarily, it counts against a philosophical thesis that it disagrees with common sense. But common sense is not infallible: it is not a final court of appeals. It is one philosophical standpoint among many that are possible. Common sense, too, must be put to the test of reasoned criticism.

Here are some important questions to ask about any claim you use in your arguments:

* Is it clear what claim is being made?
* Is it consistent with experience and perception? What is the relevant evidence?
* Does it actually reflect what is true of the world?
* Is it reasonable/adequate to an impartial third party? Are biases and prejudices avoided?
* Is it ambiguous, obscure, vague, internally contradictory, relating ideas that are mutually exclusive?
* Is it consistent with other statements already accepted? If not which statement(s) must be re-evaluated?
* Are there exceptions or counterexamples to the claim?
* Does the statement have unacceptable consequences, or introduce inconsistency or contradiction?
* Does the statement fit with common uses of language? If not, define terms and justify your usage.
* Are there alternative statements that are equally or more clearly reasonable? Is there a better way to make the point clear and acceptable?

4. *Informal Fallacies*

Apart from the formal mistakes of reasoning (i.e., invalid arguments) that we have already discussed, there many types of faulty reasoning that are not just a matter of the argument's form. In this section we will discuss some common informal fallacies that you should avoid.

Equivocation: Sometimes a claim can be true on one reading or interpretation and false on another. Very often, a key term or phrase will turn up repeatedly in an argument and, in order for the argument to be valid, it must have the same meaning throughout. Of course, you want all your premises to be true. But sometimes the only way all the premises can be true is if we read one premise with one meaning and another premise with a second and different meaning. To do this is to equivocate. Equivocation is one type of informal fallacy and must be avoided. Consider the following argument.

1. Only men are rational animals.	1. All R's are M's.
2. No women are men.	2. No W's are M's.
	———————
3. Therefore, No women are rational.	3. No W's are R's.

The fact that we are led from apparently true premises to a patently false conclusion suggests that there is a problem with this argument. However, this argument fits one of the valid forms of argument. Since the argument is formally valid, the problem must lie in the content—in one (or more) of the premises. If "men" in premise 1 means "humans" (including both men and women)—the interpretation required to make it true—then premise 2 is false. If we interpret "men" in premise 2 so that *it* comes out true (i.e., "men" = "males"), then premise 1 comes out false. There is no *single* interpretation on which both premises come out true. We actually have our choice between saying the argument is invalid or unsound. If we interpret "men" the same way in both premises, the argument is valid, but not sound, because one premise must be false. If we allow the equivocation, the argument is invalid.

Begging the Question: An argument begs the question when a premise of the argument is simply a restatement (perhaps cleverly-disguised) of the conclusion. The argument merely moves in a circle and says the same thing twice. A very simple example is: "Learning is important because everyone should acquire knowledge."

Criticizing an argument as being question-begging can be a difficult and subtle business, for a person will rarely take the intended conclusion as an explicit premise (e.g., "Abortion is wrong because abortion is immoral.") If the conclusion is used as a premise at all, it is much more likely to be merely *implicit* in the argument, and it can be tricky to unearth implicit premises. Here is an example of an argument that may seem to be sound but which begs the question:

1. An act without the intention of the agent should not be punished.
2. An involuntary act is an act without the intention of the agent.
3. Therefore, an involuntary act should not be punished.

That this argument begs the question becomes apparent when we realize that the phrase "act without the intention of the agent" just means "involuntary act," hence the first premise and the conclusion amount to the same claim, and no progress has been made.

Post hoc fallacy: The assumption that merely because two events occur together, or in a time sequence, one is the cause and the other the effect; e.g., "He remembered to put the rabbit's foot in his pocket, so naturally he won the race."

False dilemma **(or the fallacy of black and white thinking):** The assumption is improperly made that an issue has only two sides, or that there are only two alternatives in a situation; e.g., "People are either Christians or atheists."

Argumentum ad ignorantium: The argument that what one person asserts is true because another person cannot disprove it, or that an assertion is false because another cannot prove it to be true; e.g., "God exists, because you cannot prove that He does not."

Argumentum ad hominem: The assumption that if you discredit the person, you thereby discredit his or her argument; e.g., "I don't care what Thompson said about that company's stock. That guy is a money-grubbing creep!"

Hypothesis contrary to fact: The claim that one can know with certainty what *would have* happened if a past event or condition had been different; e.g., "If only my father had been rich, I would be a successful surgeon today."

False obversion: The misuse of contrasts and opposites. The position that if a statement is true, its opposite must, therefore, be false; e.g., "Most children learn easily; therefore, most adults learn with difficulty."

False conversion: The switching of subject and predicate in a statement or proposition with the result that the new statement does not meet the requirements for correct reasoning; e.g., "All patriots salute the flag; therefore, all who salute the flag are patriots."

Reification: The practice of treating a concept or abstraction as if it were a thing (often material) with a life or power of its own; e.g., "Technology will turn all of us into machines."

Fallacy of the straw man: The strategy of attacking a proposal indirectly by setting up and destroying a substitute proposal that is more vulnerable, but beside the point; e.g., "How can I possibly receive a good education at that college when their parking is always overcrowded?"

5. *Inductive Arguments*

Up to this point we have been concerned with deductive reasoning. In deductive reasoning, if the argument is valid and the premises are true, we can be *certain* that the conclusion is true as well. The premises of an inductive argument do not provide conclusive support for (do not entail) the conclusion. Instead, they confer some degree of probability less than certainty on the conclusion. Inductive arguments are never deductively valid; the truth of the premise(s) does not guarantee the truth of the conclusion. Here is an example of an inductive argument:

1. Ten abnormally wet winters on the Pacific coast were preceded by El Ninos.
2. Therefore, El Ninos cause wet winters.

The conclusion *could* be false even if the premise were true. But just because this argument is not deductively valid does not mean it is totally worthless. There can still be "good" inductive arguments—that is, arguments which make their conclusion *probable* to some degree—but we cannot use the formal concepts of validity and soundness to evaluate them. There are many claims for which we do not have conclusive reasons; nevertheless they may be true, and we are justified in asserting them to the degree that we have evidence which supports them. The *inductive probability* of an argument is the likelihood that its conclusion is true assuming the premises are true. Deductive validity is an "all or nothing" property—an argument is either valid or not. Inductive strength, on the other hand is a matter of degrees. Inductive arguments can range in strength from extremely weak to very strong.

You are already familiar with inductive reasoning from some of its common uses: e.g., learning from experience by classifying things into kinds, and discovering how these kinds or classes relate to one another. Inductive reasoning allows us to make predictions and generalizations that go beyond our actual experience. There are six main types of inductive argument, but you are likely to come across or need only three of these types: *inductive generalization, statistical syllogism*, and *analogical arguments.*

1. *Inductive generalization* helps us frame expectations on the basis of our knowledge of the past or on observations already made. This type of argument allows us to draw a conclusion about an entire population based on what we know about a portion (or sample) of that population. Here is an example:

1. 67 percent of the State students surveyed receive some financial aid.
2. Therefore, 67 percent of all State students receive some financial aid.

This argument moves from a claim about a sample to a claim about the total population (a generalization). The argument clearly isn't valid; its strength depends (largely) on the size and representativeness of the sample of students (the sample is all the students surveyed).

2. Here is an example of induction by *statistical syllogism*:

1. 67 percent of all State students receive some financial aid.
2. Petra is a student at State.
3. Therefore, Petra (probably) receives some financial aid.

In this case the argument moves from a generalization to a claim about a particular member of the population. Here, the larger the percentage of State students receiving financial aid, the stronger the argument.

3. Since most philosophical questions are conceptual rather than factual, the vast majority of arguments you will examine or construct will be deductive arguments. However, one type of inductive argument is sometimes particularly useful in Philosophy. *Analogical arguments* assert that what is true of a sample of a certain class is true of another member of that class. Another version of this type of argument asserts that what is true of all members of one class is true of all members of another, similar class. In both cases, the argument turns on the (alleged) similarity between those things in the first

class and the individual or things in the second class. Here is an example of the second type of argument:

1. Human beings should not be subject to experimentation that causes pain.
2. Animals feel pain just as humans do.
3. Therefore, animals shouldn't be subjected to painful experimentation either.

In this argument, it is suggested that human beings and animals are *relevantly similar* with respect to feeling pain, and that if experimentation on one is prohibited on that basis, then it should also be prohibited for the other. The strength of inductive analogical arguments depends largely on the strength of the analogy that is asserted to hold between the two classes in question: the stronger the analogy, the stronger the argument.

Here are some questions that are very useful for checking inductive reasoning:

*   How complete is the evidence? What proportion of the total number of cases have been examined?
*   How reliable, accurate, and objective is the evidence?
*   Is the sample representative? Are examined cases typical of the total population?
*   Have negative instances been sought out and taken into account?
*   Are there alternative theories to explain the data?
*   How strong are the alleged analogies between things or classes of things?

Chapter 3

Some Important Analytical Tools

A. *Conceptual Analysis*

There are different kinds of thinking, but the kind we will concentrate on is analytical thinking. Most philosophical issues or problems require that we think very carefully about the central concepts that figure in the question or problem. For example, if we are wondering whether humans have free will, we must analyze the concepts of "will" or "volition", and "freedom". What does it mean to say that a human action is "free" or "un-free"? Almost any course may require you to write an essay that calls for the analysis of some concept, so this chapter may prove useful in writing other types of essays as well.

A philosophical paper is, at bottom, the presentation of an argument or series of arguments on a given issue. Since your main goal is to reach and defend a conclusion, part of your task will be to establish that your conclusion is supported by a set of reasons (premises). But you also need to establish that the various claims you make are true, or at least very probably true. But it is virtually impossible to determine if a claim is true if you aren't clear what items or concepts are being referred to. For example, if you are trying to determine whether euthanasia is ever permissible, you obviously need to know what euthanasia is. Just what situations or cases does it include?

Conceptual analysis is one of the most important tools used by contemporary philosophers to evaluate claims and understand their component concepts. Conceptual analysis involves trying to specify necessary and sufficient conditions for the correct application of a concept. In definitions of concepts, necessary and sufficient conditions are indicated by the phrase "...if and only if..." (for example: "A person is a bachelor if and only if they meet certain conditions a, b and c). "If...." indicates the conditions that are sufficient for being an X, while "only if..." indicates the necessary conditions—those conditions that *must* be satisfied in order to be an X. Since it is a way of precisely defining concepts this technique is often very useful when trying to clarify concepts: "What does it mean to be an X?"

For example, suppose someone wants to know what a "bachelor" is. It would clearly not be enough to tell them that a bachelor is an unmarried male. A two-year-old boy satisfies those conditions, but we would not say that he is a bachelor. The two specified conditions are not strong enough to pick out all and only bachelors. We could strengthen the analysis by adding that bachelors are unmarried *adult* males. Is this correct? What about unmarried adult male gorillas?! We also need to specify that we are restricting the analysis to humans. What if we further added that bachelors are unmarried adult human males *who drive sports cars*? This would make the analysis *too* strong, for it will inappropriately exclude some people from the class of bachelors: you don't have to drive a sports car to be a bachelor. Be careful, then, that your analysis is neither too weak nor too strong.

Tentatively, one might propose to define "bachelor" by specifying the necessary and sufficient conditions for being a bachelor, like this: "X is a bachelor if and only if X is an unmarried male human of marriageable age." *If* this analysis is correct (what about priests? or divorcees? Are they bachelors?) then the stated conditions are jointly sufficient and individually necessary for being a bachelor. Conceptual analysis may seem a bit cumbersome or confusing at first, but it is an essential step toward precise and careful thinking.

Any conceptual analysis should avoid *circularity* if possible. An analysis is circular if the term you are analyzing (in Latin, the *analysandum*) occurs in the analysis (the *analysans*). For example, if you say that "melting" is "something that happens to a solid when it melts," your analysis is obviously circular. The analysis explains nothing unless we already know what melting is, but that was what we wanted an analysis of in the first place. When

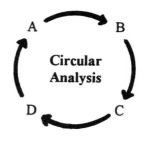

A   B

Circular
Analysis

D   C

analyzing an important concept, make sure that the analysis you offer (or are criticizing) is truly informative and avoids this type of circularity.

That said, we should note that under certain conditions, a circular analysis *can* be somewhat helpful. Suppose we have a number of concepts (A, B, C, ... Z) to analyze and A occurs in the *analysans* of B, B in the *analysans* of C, ..., and Z in the *analysans* of A so that we have come full circle. It might seem that someone who did not understand any of these notions would not be helped at all by any of these analyses, much as being told that melting is something that happens to solids when they melt is unhelpful unless you already know what melting is. If she doesn't understand any of the *analysanda,* and each *analysans* contains one of the *analysanda,* then it would seem that she has no way to break into the conceptual circle. This can sometimes happen, but usually we will have at least some understanding of one of the concepts involved and this can lead to a partial understanding of the others. This dim understanding can be further enhanced by going around the circle and seeing how each concept is connected with the others. In any case, our goal should be to analyze concepts in terms of other concepts that are clearly understood.

B. *Counterexamples*

The method of counterexample is a powerful analytic tool that is often used to refute a claim or thesis. Very simply, a counterexample is an example that runs counter to some proposition or claim. There are two types: *propositional* and *argumental.*

1. A *propositional counterexample* is an example which disproves, or is evidence against, a proposition; usually the proposition to be refuted is a universal judgment like "All ravens are black." For example, the claim "All human actions are selfish" could be refuted by pointing to a non-selfish human action; one case is all it takes. This is a refutation of a generalization by propositional counterexample.

Propositional counterexamples can also be used to refute a proposed analysis of a concept. Since a conceptual analysis proposes both necessary and sufficient conditions for being an X (e.g., a bachelor) a counterexample could be constructed to show either (1) that the analysis does not express the correct *sufficient conditions* of the concept X, or (2) that the analysis does not express the correct *necessary conditions* of the concept.

To show that a set of conditions is not sufficient for being an X you must find something that satisfies the analysis but is not an accepted instance of X. For example, if it is proposed that a bachelor is an unmarried male, you can "counterexample" the claim by pointing to a two-year-old boy, noting that even though he is an unmarried male, we would not consider him a bachelor. The proposed analysis could then be strengthened to avoid this counterexample by including the condition that the unmarried male be an adult or, better, of marriageable age. Are the conditions "unmarried male of marriageable age" (jointly) sufficient to capture all bachelors?

To show that a condition is not necessary you must find something which is an accepted instance of the concept, but which does not satisfy the proposed analysis. For example, suppose someone claimed that bachelors are unmarried males of marriageable age *who frequent singles bars*. This analysis is too strong: there are plenty of bachelors who don't go to singles bars. So frequenting singles bars is *not* a necessary condition of being a bachelor.

2. An *argumental counterexample* targets an argument or inference, instead of a single claim. Suppose someone argues:

1. If Cindy took a bath, then she got wet.
2. Cindy did not take a bath.
3. Therefore, Cindy did not get wet.

This argument might be tempting, but it is invalid. That it *is* invalid could be shown by constructing a second argument that has the same structure, and which clearly reveals the fallacious inference. For example,

1. If Lassie had been a dachshund, then she'd have been a dog.
2. Lassie was not a dachshund.
3. Therefore, Lassie was not a dog.

The premises of this argument are true (a conditional statement is true whenever the antecedent is false) but the conclusion is obviously false, hence the argument is invalid. Since this argument is invalid, and the first argument has the same form (If P, then Q; Q; therefore, P) it must be invalid as well, even though at first glance it may have looked like a good argument. Both of these arguments commit what is called the fallacy of "affirming the consequent." Constructing an argumental counterexample is a useful way of showing that an invalid argument *is* invalid.

If you are able to produce a counterexample that refutes a claim or theory, then you have done something quite significant. But since the goal of philosophical inquiry is truth, it would be even more significant if the counterexample itself suggested a way to modify the position so that it is sound, or if it suggested an alternate definition or theory that is more adequate. (This is what we did above with the claim that a bachelor is an unmarried male. Your young nephew is a counterexample, since he is an unmarried male but we wouldn't say that he is a bachelor. This suggests that we should include a condition concerning age.) Importantly, you can use the method of counterexample to strengthen your own claims and arguments: test them by trying to imagine possible counterexamples.

Unfortunately, there are no simple rules for thinking up counterexamples. Some people are very good at it, and others struggle. It takes an active and insightful imagination and a lot of persistence. You may have to run through a lot of possible examples before you discover one that actually refutes the target claim or inference, instead of being just another confirming instance of it. Nevertheless, the counterexample is one of the most powerful techniques used in philosophical argumentation.

C. *Dilemmas*

Facing a dilemma is like being between a rock and a hard place. A dilemma usually involves setting out alternatives that are somehow incompatible or unpleasant. Here is a dilemma allegedly offered by the general who set fire to the library of Alexandria:

> If these books merely repeat what is in the Koran they are superfluous; if they report something other than what is contained in the Koran, they are deceptive. But they must either repeat, or report something other than, what is contained in the Koran. Therefore, the books are either superfluous or deceptive.

Notice that the premises are two hypothetical claims (or *conditionals:* "if__ then__" statements) and a *disjunction* ("either__or__"). The form of the argument is this:

> 1. If P then Q.
> 2. If R then S.
> but 3. Either P or R.
> therefore 4. Either Q or S.

Dilemmas can be useful for setting out a problem. For example:

If determinism is true, then people aren't responsible for their actions; (and) if determinism is not true, then humans don't cause their own actions. But either determinism is true or it isn't. Therefore, either humans aren't responsible for their actions or they don't cause their own actions.

Both of the possible conclusions are unpleasant. Since the argument is valid, the only way to avoid the unpleasant conclusion is to deny one or another of the premises. Showing that the disjunctive premise is false is called "going between the horns of the dilemma" (there is some overlooked third option). You might also try to show directly that one of the "if___ then___" statements) is false. This strategy is called "grabbing the dilemma by the horns."

D. *Reductio Ad Absurdum*

Despite the intimidating Latin name, *reductio ad absurdum* (literally, to reduce to absurdity) is a common and fairly simple argumentative strategy. You already know how to do it. Roughly, if you can show that your opponent's position is incoherent—leads to a contradiction—you have shown the position (or at least part of it) is false. *Reductio* arguments exploit the truth-preserving character of logical entailment: from truths, only truths follow. Thus, if a claim entails something false, then that claim must be false.

The strategy of a *reductio* argument, then, is to assume, for the sake of the argument, the *opposite* of what you want to prove, and show that that assumption (when combined with a few other premises) leads to a falsehood. It is obviously very important that you establish that the entailed claim is false. You can do this by an appeal to evidence, but the surest way is to derive a *contradiction* from the assumption. Contradictions—compound claims of the form "P & not P"—are *necessarily* false; e.g., "The light is on and the light is not on". Be careful, however: some claims that do not have precisely this form can still be contradictory (e.g., "Some Republicans are liberal, but no liberals are Republicans" [in logic, "but" means "and"]). In formal logic, *reductio* arguments always rely on the derivation of a contradiction.

```
1. Assume not Q
2. Premise
3. Premise

   .    .
   .    .
   .    .

n. R and not R        <— contradiction
   _____

n+1.  Q
```

Reductios exhibit the general form illustrated in the box above (Q is the claim to be proved, R is a derived proposition). The dots between the initial premises and the contradiction may include whatever valid inferences from the initial premises that are needed to generate the conclusion. Since the assumption of not Q leads to a contradiction (and all contradictions are necessarily false), not Q must be false. Therefore, Q must be true.

A classic example of *reductio ad absurdum* is Anselm's ontological argument for the existence of God. Anselm wants to prove that God—the greatest conceivable being—must exist. He begins by assuming the opposite of what he wants to prove, and will show how that assumption leads to a contradiction:

1. Suppose that God does not exist.
2. If the greatest conceivable being does not exist, then something greater than it can be conceived, namely, something that has all the properties of the greatest conceivable being plus the property of existence.
3. But then the greatest conceivable being is *not* the greatest conceivable being.
4. However, the greatest conceivable being *is* the greatest conceivable being (obviously!).
5. Therefore, God exists [= it is not true that God does not exist].

The assumption at (1) (the opposite of the desired conclusion) leads to the contradiction between (3) and (4), so that assumption must be false.

Do not become disoriented by the fact that you have to assume the *opposite* of what you want to prove in order to construct a *reductio* argument. This does not mean that you endorse or believe that assumption; you are merely using it to prove what you do believe. Nor does a *reductio* commit its author to the derived falsehood or contradiction. The author is merely pointing to the absurdity that follows from rejecting his position.

E. *Strength of Propositions*

Some claims are "stronger" (or "weaker") than others. The relative strength of propositions is measured in terms of entailment:

A proposition P is stronger than a proposition Q if and only if P entails Q and Q does not entail P.

"P entails Q" means that if P is true then Q must be true as well. The claim "All human actions are motivated by self-interest" is stronger than "Some human actions are motivated by self-interest," because if the first claim is true, then the second must also be true, but not vice versa. Two propositions are equally strong if each entails the other (e.g., "Horses are creatures with hearts," and "Horses are creatures with kidneys"; if one of these is true then so is the other).

If there are no entailment relations between two propositions, then they cannot be compared in terms of strength, even if superficially one sounds stronger than another. For example, "Some human actions are selfish," does not entail, and is not entailed by "All horses are creatures with hearts." These claims are about such diverse topics that they have no bearing on each other, and so cannot be compared in terms of strength. Generally, if one proposition is stronger than another, then it requires more or better evidence to prove it. But if they cannot be compared in terms of strength, then there is no clear-cut way of predicting which proposition will require more or better evidence.

The question of the strength of propositions is important for several reasons. First, it would be imprudent to use premises that are stronger than is necessary to prove your conclusion, because the stronger you make the claim, the more difficult it becomes to defend it. Also, if you rely on a proposition that is stronger than you need and you fail to defend it, your audience may infer that your position is untenable, even if there is some weaker proposition that *is* defensible and entails your conclusion. On the other hand, your premises should not be too weak, for then they won't entail the conclusion: your argument will be invalid.

Knowing the strength of a proposition is also useful when you are evaluating an opposing position, or when entertaining possible objections to your own view. A corollary about strength is that the stronger a claim is, the less it takes to refute it; and the weaker a claim is, the more it takes to refute it. So, the claim *"All* human actions are selfish," is a very strong claim. If you could show that some human actions (even one) are not selfish, then you would successfully refute the claim.

Stronger claims	Weaker claims
* are more difficult to defend * are more easy to refute	* are more easy to defend * are more difficult to refute

There is no general formula for determining how much evidence is needed to prove or adequately support a thesis. It depends both on the strength of the thesis and on the needs of your audience. It is up to you to provide as much evidence as is necessary to inform and convince your audience.

Chapter 4

Some Other Philosophical Virtues:

Before we discuss the actual composition process we should mention a number of virtues that you should strive for in your thinking and writing. Two of the most important qualities philosophical writing should have are consistency and coherence. Three other important virtues of good philosophical writing are continuity, conciseness, and clarity.

A. *Consistency*

In the course of your essay you will make a large number of claims covering many different facets of your subject. You must be careful that what you say on one page does not contradict or conflict with what you say on another. In short, you must take special care to ensure that your essay is *consistent*. Consistency is a property of sets or groups of sentences (e.g., all the claims in your paper).

> *A set of claims is CONSISTENT if and only if it is possible for all of them to be true at the same time.*

It may seem quite a simple thing to develop a consistent position, but experience suggests that beginning students actually find this very difficult. It is surprising how often a student will assert that *P*, and later unwittingly assert *not P*. More often the inconsistency is less obvious: instead of blatantly

35

asserting *not P*, it may be claimed that *R*, and the student does not see that *R entails not P*. Inconsistency is one of the clearest indications that the author has not carefully thought through his or her position, taking care to determine the logical consequences of what is claimed.

Sometimes complex claims can be internally inconsistent or self-contradictory. The clearest example is a single proposition that asserts "(Both) P and not P". Again, the contradictory nature of such an assertion is usually not this obvious, and care must be taken to purge your essay of this kind of mistake.

Inconsistency of any sort is especially damaging because, once the reader is confronted with it, it becomes anybody's guess which of the two inconsistent claims the author is committed to. Either way there is trouble, for not everything that is said can be true at the same time.

To make matters worse, if your view is not consistent, *it entails any and every assertion whatsoever*, including "Socrates is a humpback whale," and "The moon was made in Wisconsin." By employing the strategy of *reductio ad absurdum* it can be shown that *anything at all* follows logically from a contradiction, including other contradictions! (Can you see how to do it? Consult any good logic text to see how this surprising result is obtained, or ask your instructor to show you.) Suffice it to say that inconsistency and contradiction are to be avoided at all costs.

B. *Coherence*

An individual sentence can be incoherent in the sense that it is altogether meaningless. However, as we shall use the term, incoherence results when the parts of an essay do not fit together to form a coherent whole. This can happen in several ways. Incoherence can arise when a meaningful sentence is placed in a context where it doesn't belong. A sentence or paragraph is incoherent when it does not 'hang together' with the surrounding text. An entire essay is incoherent to the degree that it is infected with incoherent components.

"Directionless" papers—papers that ramble about, failing to follow a clear train of thought from one point to another—are also incoherent. The content of the paper may be quite good, but if the student does not present the material in such a way that the reader sees how that material establishes her conclusion, then her essay will be much weaker than it might have been.

C. *Continuity*

One way to eliminate incoherence is to strive for continuity. Ideas should follow each other in a rigorous, formal, and logical way; one part of the essay should flow smoothly from the preceding part and into the next. You have probably heard Winston Churchill's well-worn, but basically sound advice to tell your audience what you're going to do, do it, and then tell them what you've done. Your essay should be full of "road signs" letting your reader know where he or she is at all times. Use Churchill's advice within the various parts of the essay to show how the various parts fit together. In this regard you should pay attention to transitions between paragraphs and sections. This will help to make clear the organization of the ideas and reveal the structure of the overall argument. This forces *you* to be clear about these matters, in addition to making it easier for the reader to understand and evaluate your essay.

Notify your reader of your direction and purpose by filling your essay with signposts like, 'I shall begin with...,' 'I will now argue that...,' and 'I conclude that..."' These transitional phrases are usually most at home at the beginning of paragraphs and show how the major ideas of the essay fit together. Some other transitional expressions are 'therefore,' 'consequently,' 'further,' 'furthermore,' 'moreover,' and 'in addition.'

In order for the flow of information or thoughts to be continuous throughout a paragraph, you might think of each sentence as consisting of a subject and a predicate (e.g., 'A-B'). Each sentence should begin with a subject that has been encountered in a previous sentence or paragraph. Thus, to maintain a continuous flow of information, try to construct your paragraphs with one of the following forms (or any of the variations that can be constructed from them):

A-B		A-B		A-B
A-C	or	B-C	or	A-C
A-D		C-D		C-D
A-E		D-E		C-E

D. *Clarity*

Clarity of expression depends on the careful selection and precise use of words. Vague or 'high-falutin' language is *not* a sign of philosophical insight or a superior intellect. Critical thinking depends on the consistent organization of the units of language (words, sentences, paragraphs) into ordered and intelligible discourse. Pay attention to grammar and syntax. Be wary of divergent uses of words, multiple meanings, and ambiguity. Avoid relying on metaphor or analogy, and try to stay away from unexplained jargon. Use simple, clear, straightforward language to say just what you mean. Remember, you are trying to persuade your reader that your thesis is correct. You cannot hope to accomplish this if your writing leaves the reader confused or unsure of your meaning.

Pay attention to your writing and try very hard to be objective—ask yourself how someone who came to your writing 'cold' would react to it. One technique that is especially useful here is to take a break from your writing and come back to it fresh. Carefully read what you've written to see if it says what you want it to. Is it clear? Is your terminology appropriate? Do the thoughts flow from one to the next? Is what you've written plausible?

Remember that clarity is relative to an audience. An exposition of Hegel's doctrine of dialectic that is clear to a Hegel scholar may not be clear to someone who has never heard of Hegel. Whether your writing is clear or not depends (in part) on what you may rightfully presuppose about your audience's beliefs or knowledge. Avoid at all costs the tendency to fall back on the excuse, "Well, the instructor will know what I mean." If you aren't clearly *expressing* what you mean, the odds are that your reader *won't* know what you mean.

A common student retort (after the paper has been graded) is, "But that's what I *meant* by this!" Remember that your instructor is not a 'mind reader' and does not have access to any of the thoughts that you do not carefully put on paper. This is why it can be unwise to write specifically for your instructor; there is the danger of assuming that he or she knows what you're up to even though it's not on paper. (See also Chapter 6, B: "Audience".)

E. *Conciseness*

Another virtue desired in philosophical writing is conciseness. Concise writing packs a lot of information into a brief space. Write no more than is necessary in order to achieve your objectives. But be careful: like all good things, conciseness can be overdone. Don't strive so much for conciseness that you deprive your essay of the development that a point may need to be clear and convincing.

Chapter 5

The Writing Process

Now that you are armed with an arsenal of logical and conceptual tools and have chosen a topic, it is time to consider the actual nuts and bolts of composing your essay. There are many books on composition and much of their advice is applicable to philosophical writing as well; look for them in your library. English departments in many colleges operate a writing center that offers literature or even personal assistance. Take advantage of the resources available to you.

Good philosophical writing does not happen overnight; it can only emerge from sustained reflection and refinement. Consequently, the most important single bit of advice I could give is, "Start right away!" As soon as you know the assignment, take at least the initial steps toward getting started. This is the best way to avoid both "writer's block" and the unnecessary panic of discovering that the paper is due next week, and you haven't even begun. Know your due dates and set up a schedule outlining the various things you need to do and desired completion dates for those tasks. Construct a reasonable schedule and try to stick to it, but be prepared to make adjustments as necessary.

A. *Getting Started*

You must first know what your assignment is. This includes knowing what type of paper you are to write, its desired length, the goals of the paper, and the criteria that will be used to evaluate the paper. If you remain unsure about any of these points, ask your instructor for more information.

1. *Types of Philosophy Papers*

The type of paper you will be asked to write will depend on the type of class you are in and on your instructor's preferences. *Compare and contrast papers* show how two views, theories, or philosophical positions are alike and how they differ. Such papers may or may not invite you to make your own criticisms and evaluations of the views in question. The purpose of *analysis papers* is to identify and examine some elements or aspects of a concept, theory, article, or a philosopher's system of thought. Research papers in philosophy usually survey important views that have been published on a certain topic. The purpose of *summary papers* is to clearly restate and explain someone else's view in your own words. Many instructors favor the *thesis defense paper*, in which the student takes a position on a question or issue and develops an argument (or set of arguments) in support of that thesis.

We shall focus on the thesis defense paper for several reasons. First, thesis defense papers are more commonly assigned. Second, I think this type of paper is far more interesting for students to write (and for instructors to read). Third, these papers provide the best opportunity for students to hone their skills of careful argumentation. Finally, thesis defense papers invite students to develop their *own* views, rather than to merely regurgitate or comment on the views of others.

2. *Criteria of Evaluation*

Since you will be raising a question and then providing and defending an answer to that question, your paper will be evaluated largely in terms of how well you do that. To succeed you must present, develop, and defend at least one *good argument* in favor of your position. One *good* philosophical argument is enough, but you may find that you have a number of different reasons for taking the position you do. Take care to distinguish the different arguments.

It is not enough, however, merely to present your positive argument(s). In almost any philosophical debate there is room for argumentation of both sides of the issue. Since your job is to persuade the reader that your position is correct, you will have to examine and try to refute plausible objections that opponents might make to your argument. Moreover, you will likely need to attack an opponent's own arguments to show that *their* position is not better than yours. If you are to succeed in persuading your reader that your position is correct, you need to make sure that all your arguments (both offensive and defensive) are as strong as possible. Make sure you are familiar with the principles of argumentation discussed earlier in this book.

In addition to strong arguments, you should also strive for a *balanced and thoughtful presentation* of the issues. Make sure that you cover the most important issues, arguments, or theories that are pertinent to your question. This means that you will have to do some reading and research to familiarize yourself with the literature on your topic.

Be careful to *organize* the presentation of ideas in the clearest and most persuasive fashion. The reader should always understand why you are discussing something, and how it fits in with your overall position. Use transition sentences to indicate how one part of the paper leads to the next.

Always strive for accuracy and truth. Try to make and rely only on claims that are true or at least well-supported. Accurately present the arguments of philosophers or others who may have written on your topic; defeating a misrepresentation or distortion of someone's position is defeating only a "straw man," leaving their real position standing.

Few instructors will expect students to come up with a thesis and/or arguments that are completely original, but *originality* is also an important criterion of good philosophical writing. It is most important to show that you have thought carefully and deeply about the issues, and have come to your position based on an evaluation of the available evidence and arguments.

Some instructors are very fussy about *grammar, punctuation, and neatness*, while for others this has only an indirect impact on the overall quality of the paper. Careful writing is extremely important, especially in philosophy, where we are often concerned with difficult and subtle concepts, questions, and theories. Poor writing makes it difficult to understand what you are trying to say. This, in turn, makes it difficult to determine whether what you are saying is true.

These are some of the main standards your paper may be expected to meet. Know what is expected of you, then try to meet those goals.

3. *Choosing a Topic*

Once you know what the assignment is and what sort of paper you are to write, you must choose a topic. Your instructor may offer a list of possible topics from which you are to choose, or you may be given the latitude to choose your own. Choosing a topic on your own can be a difficult task. One common mistake is to choose overly broad topics like "The Problem of Determinism" or "Euthanasia." Such topics are very problematic. First, they are too broad to be handled in short papers; either of these would be better addressed in an entire book. Instead, focus on one aspect of the problem of euthanasia, or a subset of euthanasia cases (e.g., voluntary active euthanasia). Pick a topic that is both interesting to you and manageable; you don't have to solve all the world's philosophical problems in one short paper! On the other hand, don't pick a topic that is so narrow or trivial as to be uninteresting, e.g., "Is Murder Morally Wrong?"

Second, such topic/titles as those above are non-committal and hence uninformative. They give the reader no indication at all what aspect of the problem will be addressed or what position the author will argue for. A better strategy is to formulate your topic/title as a short, narrowly focused question: "Is Voluntary Active Euthanasia Morally Permissible?" This clearly identifies the content of the paper, and prepares the reader to encounter your answer to the question—your thesis, which should be stated in the opening paragraph. Alternatively, you could formulate your topic as a short declarative sentence, e.g. "Voluntary Active Euthanasia is Morally Permissible." Such titles may not be very catchy or clever, but they are efficient and informative, which is far more important.

Whether your instructor requires this or not, it is a good idea to clear your topic with your instructor as soon as you can. Your instructor can provide invaluable advice on formulating or narrowing your topic and devising a plan of action for research and writing. Getting clearance can also prevent the disastrous situation of writing a paper on a topic that your instructor will ultimately find objectionable or problematic in some way. Avoid such false-starts (or failed attempts) by checking with your instructor before you get too far along on the project.

4. *Refining Your Question*

Once you have chosen your general topic, the first thing you must do is refine your question. This is something that all philosophers must do when confronted with a philosophical problem, but it is also a very good way to begin getting clear about the issues—especially if you start out not having any idea what to think. Suppose your topic is formulated in terms of a question, for example, "Are any human actions free?" The philosophical question being posed here is obviously not whether any of the things people do don't have to be paid for! That is not the relevant sense of "free." Instead, the question asks whether any actions are freely chosen and done without coercion.

Your initial response may be to say, "What a stupid question! Obviously, yes!" Beware if you find yourself reacting in this way. You may be over-looking something important; indeed, you may have missed the point of the question altogether. Remember that questions which have one meaning (and hence one answer) in ordinary language can often take on a technical or more complex meaning when considered philosophically. Besides, if someone seriously raises a question that seems to you to have an *obvious* answer, she probably has some reason to think that the answer is *not* so obvious after all, and you should try to discover what her reasons are. Don't jump to conclusions.

In the case of human action, it is often pointed out that human actions, just like any other events in the physical world, are the effects of preceding causes, so in what sense are they free? What could possibly by meant by "free human action"? And which of these meanings reveals the philosophical problem? Distinguish the various plausible interpretations and show how they result in different questions. Then make clear to your audience which of these questions you will attempt to answer.

By showing how your question leads to a philosophical problem you motivate the entire essay and give your reader a reason to be interested in what you have to say. Sometimes a philosophical dispute festers on merely because the disputants mistakenly think that they are trying to answer the same question, when in fact they are talking at cross-purposes. Carefully formulating one's question can sometimes be half the work of answering it. As you can see, one of your first tasks is to clarify important terms in your question. Words in philosophy can be used much differently than in normal usage, so define important terms that may be ambiguous or controversial. Select definitions from readings or class, or carefully create your own (avoid using standard dictionaries). Define any technical terms. A good rule of thumb is: if you didn't know what it meant when you first read or heard it, define it.

B. *The Body*

After choosing and refining your topic, you may find that:
- you have no idea what your position is or will be;
- you know the answer you want to give, but do not how to develop or defend it;
- you may have some vague thoughts about how to make your case; or
- you may have well-ordered thoughts, including the core of an argument.

Whatever your starting position, it will be very helpful to have an organizational structure to guide your compositional efforts. Treat the task of writing as you would chisel a statue out of stone. Do it in stages, with each successive stage bringing you closer to the final work.

Since you are being asked to write about a philosophical problem, I suggest that you *conceptualize your paper as having three major parts*: in Part 1 you *raise the question*; in Part 2 you *give your answer;* in Part 3 you *present and defend your argument* for that answer. These parts will not all be of equal length; part 3 will by far be the longest. The others could be quite short.

1. *Brainstorming*

Once you have defined key terms, clarified your question, and set out the issues you will need to address, your position may readily reveal itself. If it doesn't, don't despair; you will still have done some extremely important work without which you might never be able to settle on a position.

Some students are inclined to panic at this stage: "How am I ever going to get 10 pages out of this!?" Don't panic! Whatever considerations that motivated you to choose your topic probably included some intuitions—vague though they may be—as to what you think will be your answer. Try to capture those intuitions, then you can begin refining, developing, and defending them. Doing this very early is extremely important.

One good way to find your direction is to use the technique of conceptual note-taking or "brainstorming." It can also help to forestall the fear that often leads to writer's block. Basically, it is uncensored and uncriticized writing. The strategy here is to make notes of anything and everything that comes to mind concerning your question. Write down whatever thoughts you have about the topic, even if you are just raising questions for yourself. Even having nothing to say is a place to start: "What is X anyway?" "How is X to be distinguished from or related to other things?" The point is not to try to be right, but to unearth raw ideas which can later be evaluated and organized in preparation for a first draft. You may want to physically isolate these thoughts on index cards (or different computer pages) for easy arrangement once you have begun evaluating them.

Another perhaps even less intimidating way to begin is to talk with a classmate or friend about your topic/question and your initial thoughts about it. Explain to them (as well as you can) what the question or problem is and discuss some of the things you think might be relevant. Tracing the contours of your conversation—make notes while you talk!—can provide the beginnings of your paper. Of course, you'll later want to critically evaluate and sort out these initial thoughts, discarding some and developing others, but you'll be on your way toward an outline.

2. *Outlining and Structure*

Developing and writing from an outline is absolutely essential to good philosophical writing. Your first outline could be as simple as three sentences: question, answer, and reason for thinking this answer is correct. In fact, it is a very good idea to try to write a "three sentence paper" as soon as you have chosen your topic. This is a good way to overcome writer's block. Then you can begin to fill in the exposition and/or argument in each part.

I cannot stress enough the importance of constructing outlines and using them to produce a draft. A philosophy paper is basically a long, complex argument that provides and defends an answer to a question. Outlining the issues and your position makes the content of your essay clear by revealing the structure of the thoughts. Every important claim that you make should have a place in your outline, and its relation to the other claims should be illustrated by its position in the outline. In short, the outline tells you not only what you want to say, but also how the various pieces of the puzzle fit together to form a coherent and persuasive whole.

You should not think of outlining as being useful only prior to the actual writing. Once you have produced a draft you should try to construct an outline of what you have actually written and check it against the outline you started from. This is a very useful way of making sure that you have said what you wanted to say. Did you leave out anything important? Have you included material that is irrelevant or unnecessary?

One of the most common sources of disagreement between instructors and students arises when the instructor complains that the student has left out, or not adequately developed, an important point. Frequently, the reply is, "But I *did* that!!" All too often the student only *thinks* he or she has done it. The best way to avoid this problem is to check the content of your paper by carefully and objectively outlining what you have written. (Students who have outlined their essays *after* grading have expressed considerable surprise at what they have found.) It is all too easy to think that you have made or sufficiently developed a point when you haven't because you are writing "from inside your own head."

In addition to constructing an argument (or arguments) for your thesis—the "positive" part of the paper—you will need to defend your position against likely objections or challenges. You may also need to discuss and criticize the arguments put forward by those who disagree with you. This is the "negative" or destructive part of the paper. Doing one or both of these things helps to persuade the reader that yours is not just one of many possible positions, but that yours is the best, or most plausible view.

Which of these things should you do first? How should you order these different components of the argument? There is no set answer to these questions. Some topics will lend themselves to one presentation, but often, any of several different argumentative strategies may be effectively employed. Here are three general orderings of tasks that could be used (other orderings are, of course, possible):

1. Positive argument(s)
2. Objections and replies
3. Competing arguments
4. Criticism and comparison with your position

1. Survey of competing arguments
2. Criticism of these
3. Positive argument(s)
4. Objections and replies

1. Positive argument #1
2. Objections and replies
3. Positive argument #2
4. Objections and replies
etc.
n. Competing arguments, criticisms, and comparison

You can't hope to write a good paper until you've carefully worked through the issues. Developing a thorough and coherent outline is crucial to a good paper, for it is here that both you, and your reader, see how all the pieces of the puzzle fit together. If they *don't* fit together you have more work to do! With a good outline in hand, writing the paper should be mainly a matter of putting these core ideas into readable and persuasive prose.

a. *Sample Outlines*

Here are three examples of actual outlines done by students. The first is a fairly good outline, while the other two have some fairly substantial flaws.

Topic/Title: Is Capital Punishment Morally Acceptable Punishment?

I. Introduction
QUESTION: Is capital punishment a morally acceptable form of punishment?
ANSWER: I argue that CP is not morally acceptable.
II. Body
A. Those favoring and opposing CP have many arguments supporting their viewpoints. I will take the position of an abolitionist of CP. CP is a severe form of punishment that, I will argue, does not fit into any acceptable aim of punishment.
B. The main aims or purposes of punishment are:
   1. reform
   2. retribution
   3. prevention
   4. deterrence
I will show that CP fails to satisfy any of these aims.
   1. Some people hold that the aim of CP as reform is to induce the criminal to conform to the rules and standards of society.
      a. I don't agree with this claim: reform of the criminal is not possible because he or she will have been executed.
   2. Retribution refers to punishment where offenders are made to suffer the same pain that they have caused ("an eye for an eye"). Supporters of CP commonly use this argument.
      a. However, this is merely an attempt to justify the murder of a criminal, which is motivated by the desire for revenge.
      b. To execute a person out of this motive is unworthy of a civilized society.

3. One might attempt to justify CP on the ground that it is a suitable preventive, ensuring that the criminal does not repeat the crime or further endanger society.

    a. However, life imprisonment without parole would ensure the protection of society without requiring us to kill a human being.

    b. Besides, studies show that released or paroled convicted murderers rarely kill again.

4. The most common argument for CP is based on its deterrent value. This means that we should punish convicted felons for the purpose of discouraging others from committing similar offenses.

    a. But there is no conclusive evidence that shows that CP really does deter violent crime.

    b. People don't think about the possibility of capital punishment when they kill.

    c. There are also people who just don't care about what happens to them.

III. In conclusion, I find that CP is not morally acceptable since all the attempts to justify it by showing that it serves one of the acceptable ends of punishment fail.

This outline makes very clear what the author's question is and what position the author takes. The body of the outline also shows clearly how (s)he is going to support that position. All of the entries are complete, declarative sentences, leaving no doubt or confusion as to what the author's point is. The author shows how the parts of the paper flow logically, illustrating how the whole paper hangs together to prove the author's point.

There is, however, one significant problem with this outline. The author mistakenly thinks that by knocking down the various justifications of capital punishment that (s)he has shown that capital punishment is immoral. That claim must be defended by providing a positive argument to that effect. It is never enough merely to discredit one's opponents (one can never be sure one hasn't overlooked a successful defense of the view being attacked). One must positively argue *for* one's own position. Your goal, remember, is to convince the reader that your position is *correct*, and not merely that the opposing views are wrong.

A word of warning about the outline above: do not assume that every philosophical problem can be wrangled into exactly this structure. This outline is provided merely as an example of the *types* of things a good outline should include. The structure of your outline should be dictated by the particular issues you are confronting, and your opinion about the best way to address them.

Here are two rather poor outlines:

Outline on Sexual Libertarianism

I. What is sexual libertarianism?
   A. Definition
   B. Beliefs of sexual libertarians
II. Different views on sex:
   A. Traditional view
   B. Libertarian view
III. Arguments: points and counterpoints
   A. for sexual libertarianism
       1. sex is a private matter
       2. the influence of the sexual revolution
       3. curbing sexual freedom
       4. traditional sexual morality as hypocritical
   B. Against sexual libertarianism
       1. undermines morality
       2. sex without love
       3. undermines marriage
       4. influence on society
IV. Pros and cons of sexual libertarianism
   A. Pedophilia/coercion
       1. exploitation
       2. "scarring for life"
   B. Homosexuality
       1. Who are the gays?
       2. The unnaturalness of homosexuals
   C. Incest
       1. devastation within the family
       2. reproduction and the gene pool
V. In closing...

ABORTION: Outline

I. Is the fetus human or a person?
    A. I will discuss Callahan's view
    B. I am still researching other philosophers' opinions and will include the ones I select.
II. Woman v. Fetus
    A. Who is more important
        1. Woman has goals, love, fear, pain, etc.
        2. Fetus—potential for these things.
III. Rape
    A. I am going to read up on Roe v. Wade and include it.
    B. No matter what the circumstances, anytime a woman is sexually violated, abortion should automatically be an option for her.
IV. Abortion as birth control
    A. For married couples
        1. Repeatedly—each time pregnancy occurs
        2. Accident—one time
    B. Unmarried couples
        1. Prostitutes
        2. Teens

Both of these outlines have fairly obvious flaws. Neither outline clearly states the question being addressed or states the author's view. One- or two-word 'topic headings' are not very informative, and give no indication of what the author's position is on those matters.

Neither outline makes clear what the author's argument is or what the overall direction of the discussion will be. The outline on sexual libertarianism does point in the direction of some arguments but these are incompletely stated and there is no indication of whether the author thinks 'pro' or 'con' wins the debate. The outline on abortion is little more than some suggestions as to what the person is *going* to discuss. The outline includes neither an introduction nor a conclusion. While the person's position on the permissibility of abortion in the case of pregnancy due to rape (III, B) is stated, there is not even the hint of an argument to back it up. Moreover, the author's view of the permissibility of abortion in *other* circumstances is never stated.

Many other criticisms could be made about the specific contents of these outlines. Our goal here is simply to illustrate some of the 'rights and wrongs' that may be found in *any* outline.

3. *Research*

Depending on the assignment and on your own needs and abilities, you may want or need to provide some background information about the issues. You might, for example, wish to point out that some philosopher(s) you have read have also addressed this issue. This is where your expository skills will come in handy. Your treatment of another philosopher's work on the topic could vary from a simple mention that "Kant thought such-and-such," to a detailed exposition and critical analysis of that person's position. Of course, if you do the latter you should probably put this discussion into the body of the paper.

Exposition and explanation requires that you show that you are familiar with the views of the philosophers studied and why they hold them. It also requires that you know the structure of the arguments used to support a philosophical position, the meaning of technical terms, and the evidence for the premises. Make sure the expository parts of your essay are not *merely* exercises in paraphrasing. *Use* the findings of other thinkers to advance your own thought on the topic. Show how their view (or parts of it) can be used to support your own position. Or, show why their view is (wholly or partly) mistaken and how your own position corrects or avoids the error.

If your paper requires research, don't automatically go to the primary or secondary literature, reading anything and everything on the topic. After all, how will you know what to look for? Start by jotting down your own thoughts first; get as far as you can with an outline. You'll discover where you need more information or where you need to look for the arguments or positions of other philosophers. Beware of getting trapped in prolonged, scattershot research that prevents you from proceeding with your own work. This can clutter your mind with the thought of others, making it difficult to decide what *you* think.

a. *Reading Philosophy*

This seems an appropriate place to say a few words about reading philosophical works. It is essential that you accurately understand the works of philosophers as they pertain to the subject mater of your essay, whether you agree or disagree with them. Criticism of a philosopher's position will stand up better if you begin with the most sympathetic understanding it. If you agree with the position, again you will need a clear view of it to try to offer support at its weakest points or to make other helpful suggestions.

Here are some pointers on reading philosophy:

1. Read the whole work sympathetically. Note the organization and style, and what major problems are addressed.

2. Re-read carefully. Isolate the issues and arguments.

3. Study any pertinent section, analyzing each argument as it arises. Do outlines.

4. Try "active reading." As you read ask yourself the following questions: What problem is being addressed? Does the formulation of the problem rest on any assumptions? What assumptions are the arguments based on? Are the arguments valid and sound? How do the arguments fit into the work as a whole? Are there mistakes? If there are, are they instructive? Why were they made and how can they be corrected?

5. If you have time, re-read the whole work to get a sense of the work's overall aims and conclusions, and evaluate them for completeness and consistency.

As you can see, careful reading and analysis will obviously take some time: so start early!

If you discover that someone else has already written the same thing you want to say, footnote it. If it has already been written better than you could say it, quote it and footnote the source. If it was written before and is better and more detailed than your account, adapt it to your own needs and footnote it. If something has been written against your position but is wrong, use it as an objection, footnote it, and refute it. If you discover an opposing position that you can't refute, you may need to rethink your position. If you conclude that your view is still defensible, acknowledge the difficulty and do your best to minimize the damage to your position.

If you get stuck, research can be used to stimulate you. Consult your text, or ask your instructor, teaching assistant, or librarians for relevant resources.

b. *Use of Authority*

What makes relying on an authority acceptable is the authority's possession of good reasons for his or her views. Ultimately, the evidential value of an appeal to authority depends on the quality of the evidence offered. Just because Plato or Kant said it, doesn't automatically mean it's right. Name-dropping is just that; evidence and argument do the work.

Citing an authority can often save you the time and effort of establishing something that has already been proven. A restatement of someone else's view or result (e.g., "As Kant has shown...") is really just an abbreviation of the original argument. Beware: this use of authority is only effective if what your authority "has shown" is both known to and accepted by your reader. An appeal to authority does not relieve you of the burden of argument. If the authority's argument on which you rely is defective, then *your* argument is defective. If their argument is good, then so is yours; but don't neglect to give them credit in a footnote.

After discussing what other philosophers have said about your topic, you will want to develop your own position and distinguish it from theirs. For example, you might think that Hume's moral theory is fundamentally wrong, and that an entirely different view—yours!—is right. Show how your view differs from Hume's, and show *why* you are right and he is wrong. Or it might be that you think Hume's view is basically correct, but that there needs to be some kind of adjustment in the details of his position. Or, perhaps you think Hume's position is correct, but you have discovered an interesting new argument for it that makes it (more) convincing.

One of the most frustrating positions for some students to be in is that of thinking that So-and-So was absolutely right about some matter, and having nothing novel or particularly insightful to add. There is nothing wrong with agreeing with what someone else has already said about your topic, but the danger here is obvious: you don't want your essay to be a mere paraphrase of So-and-So's work. If it is, then, in a certain sense, it really isn't *your* essay at all. In this situation it is especially important that you demonstrate that *you* have thought about the issues for yourself, even though your conclusion agrees with X's. In fact, it is extremely rare that two people agree about *all* the details of a given position, so if you do seriously grapple with the problem, you are very likely to find points of disagreement where you can distinguish your position from theirs. Since the goal of philosophical inquiry is truth, say what you think, even if someone else thought of it first. Just make sure that you acknowledge that fact.

c. *Reference Notes*

When you refer to or quote a particular person's views, you should document the source. This can be done in a footnote, endnote, or parenthetical note within the text of your paper. Any of these methods is acceptable as long as they are done properly. The point of the reference is to enable the reader to consult the original source for verification or further study. While many people prefer endnotes, I favor footnotes since they do not require the reader to turn to the back of the paper (as with endnotes), nor do they interrupt the flow of ideas (as do parenthetical notes), thus facilitating reading. Moreover, most modern word processing programs include a footnote feature that makes footnotes easy.

In this section we provide examples of footnote entries for the types of works that you are likely to use in researching and writing your paper. Footnotes are placed at the bottom of the page separated from the text by a short line (about 2") at the left margin. Indent one tab, then place the note number slightly above the center of the line (superscript), followed by author's name, title, publication information, and page number(s).

A book by one author

[1]John Pollock, *Contemporary Theories of Knowledge* (Totowa, N.J.: Rowman & Littlefield, 1986) 174.

(If a book has co-authors, add the second author after the first: First Author and Second Author, ...)

An anthology of collected works

[2]Morris Weitz, *20th Century Philosophy: The Analytic Tradition* (New York: The Free Press, 1966) 12.

An article in an anthology

[3]Judith Jarvis Thomson, "The Right to Privacy," *Philosophical Dimensions of Privacy,* ed. Ferdinand D. Schoeman (Cambridge: Cambridge University Press, 1984) 278.

A book with an author and an editor

[4]David Hume, *An Inquiry Concerning the Principles of Morals,* ed. Charles W. Hendel (New York: Macmillan Publishing Co., 1957) 67.

A book with a translator

[5]Kant, Immanuel. *Critique of Pure Reason.* Trans. Norman Kemp Smith. New York: St. Martin's, 1933.

An article in a reference work

[6]"Personal Identity," *The Encyclopedia of Philosophy,* ed. Paul Edwards, vol. 6 (New York: Macmillan, Inc., 1967) 103.

A scholarly journal
[7]Hartry Field, "Realism and Anti-Realism about Mathematics," *Philosophical Topics* 13/1 (1982): 49.

A magazine article
[8]Ethan Nadelmann and Jann S. Wenner, "Toward a Sane National Drug Policy," *Rolling Stone* May 5, 1994: 24-25.

A newspaper article
[9]Leslie Knowlton, "A Time for Dying?" *Los Angeles Times* July 19, 1994: E1.

If you refer to a work more than once, subsequent reference notes are much shorter and easier. You merely give the author's last name, followed by the page number(s):
[10]Field 52.

If you refer to more than one work by the same author, you need to include a key word or short phrase from the work's title to avoid confusion (make sure you choose words that are unique to that title!):
[11]Hume, *Principles of Morals* 113.

d. *Bibliography*

Whether your paper includes footnotes or not, you should list the works that you relied on in researching your topic. That is, you should attach at the back of the paper a *bibliography*. Bibliographic entries contain roughly the same information as notes (minus specific page references), but in a slightly different format. *Book citations* include the following information, although some elements will sometimes be missing:

Author's last name, first name. Title (underlined or italicized). Editor or translator's name (last, first) preceded by *Ed.* or *Trans.*. Edition (3rd Ed.,), Vol. #. City of publication: Publishing Company, Year. Page number(s).

Notice that the entry employs a "hanging indent": the first line is at the left margin with subsequent lines moved to the right one Tab. Also notice the punctuation between elements.

Bibliographic entries for *periodicals* include the following information:

Author's name (last, first). "Title." Name of periodical (underlined or italicized). Series, volume, and issue number. Publication date: page numbers.

You can consult the Bibliography at the back of this *Guide* for examples of entries.

If you need more help in constructing either notes or a bibliography, consult any standard reference work on composition, such as the *Chicago Manual of Style*.

6. *Problem-Solving Techniques*

At any point in your thinking and writing it may be helpful to employ any of three very useful strategies for solving problems of any sort.

First, try to break your problem or question down into its component parts. It is always easier to solve smaller or simpler problems than larger or more complex ones.

Second, ask yourself whether your current problem is in any important way similar to other problems that you have encountered. If it is, then a solution that is similar to the one that worked for the prior problem might work for the current problem. Here, your reading and study of other philosophers' works can be especially helpful.

Third, if you know where it is you want to go in your essay, but can't quite see how to get there, try working backwards. Suppose, for example, that your desired conclusion is true. What would then have to be the case in order for it to be true? Or what other claims would entail it? By working from your starting point toward the end, and from the end back toward the beginning, you can more quickly supply the links needed to complete your essay.

7. *Developing Your Argument*

Some people will find your thesis plausible, but others will not, even after hearing your reasons for taking the position you do. However, even if everyone were to agree with your thesis, it is your duty to strengthen and defend it. Stating your thesis is only the beginning—although deciding what your thesis *is* can require a lot of careful thinking first!

Defending your thesis means that you have to construct an argument—or perhaps a series of arguments. So you will have to discover what considerations lead you to think that your answer is correct. Ask yourself (repeatedly) *why* you think your answer is correct, then state these premises in the clearest and strongest language you can.

Once you have constructed and refined your argument, you must establish that it is valid. That is, you have to show that your premises really do entail your conclusion. (Or, in the rare case of an inductive argument, you must show that it is strong; i.e., that the premises provide strong (though less than conclusive) support for the conclusion.) Then, whether the argument is deductive or inductive, you must establish that your premises really are true. Depending on the sort of claim a premise is, this can take the form of marshalling a body of conceptual evidence ("It is part of the meaning of X that...") or empirical evidence ("Scientists have discovered that...") or both. Play the skeptic: ask yourself what objections to the argument could be made. Then see if you can meet those challenges.

Essays by beginning students often suffer from a lack of substantial content. Some of the common traps that can cause this are:

* lack of serious effort.
* failure to perceive the lack of precision in ordinary language.
* failure to formulate the problem precisely or in a fruitful way.
* failure to come to grips with the problem once formulated.
* failure to note important and relevant distinctions.
* failure to get beyond a superficial approach to the issues.
* overemphasis on a single problem, or a single aspect of a problem.

Don't be afraid of making mistakes as you proceed. Nothing is chiseled in stone yet, and no one need see your initial efforts but you. If you later discover an error you will also have discovered the truth, and perhaps also arguments to defend the new position. This can actually be very helpful since others may have been tempted by the mistaken position too. If you can show both why the mistake is tempting and why it is wrong, you'll have a more powerful essay. It is more likely, though, that you will discover that your original thesis was not completely wrong-headed, but that it was too simplistic or needed qualification or refinement.

It is possible, however, that after thinking carefully about your initial position and argument(s), you find you are no longer convinced that your thesis is correct. You may discover that your argument is not as convincing as you originally thought, or that it is outweighed by considerations on the other side of the issue (the counter-arguments are stronger). Far from being the disaster many students fear, this should be welcomed as a discovery that represents growth and sophistication in one's thinking. Remember, the point of the paper is to tackle an important question and come to a defensible conclusion, even if this should turn out to be the opposite of your initial view. There is nothing wrong with changing one's mind if that is what careful evaluation of the issues requires.

You can even turn this to your advantage: explain why you were initially tempted by the original position and then show what considerations led you to abandon it in favor of the later view. You should never think that you are stuck with your initial view. Forcing yourself to defend a thesis you no longer believe defensible is intellectually dishonest, unsatisfying, and a sure recipe for disaster.

Once you have your basic position mapped out (question, answer, and reason) you can employ the technique of *successive elaboration* to put flesh on the skeleton. This technique can be fruitfully applied to all three parts of your essay, though it will be most important to the development of your thesis and its defense. You may find that you have only one main argument, or you may decide that you have several distinct (even if related) reasons for your position. In the latter case, develop separate arguments with each of the reasons at their core. One compelling argument is usually enough, but additional arguments can make a paper even more convincing. Whatever your argumentative strategy, the method of successive elaboration is particularly useful because it encourages you to proceed in an orderly and controlled manner. Each addition to the paper is prompted by the text itself.

It may be helpful to look at a concrete example of the process of developing an argument. In the late 1980's, some activist-journalists in the gay community began to publicize the homosexuality of prominent politicians and celebrities. The practice was called "outing" because these people, who were not known to be homosexual, were thus dragged "out of their closets." This practice was defended on the grounds that progress on gay issues—from lessening homophobia to gay rights to AIDS funding—could be made only by smashing stereotypes, by showing that gay people are everywhere and contributing to society. Outing was also used as a tactic to pressure closeted gay politicians into helping, rather than hurting, gay causes.

Like many people, the practice of outing may strike you as morally repugnant. But why? How could one argue that outing is morally wrong? At first glance, it looks like outing violates the outee's privacy by publicizing a very intimate and sensitive fact about the person's sexuality. So far, then, the thesis is that outing is wrong because it violates the outee's right to privacy. The missing premise, of course, is that violations of privacy are morally wrong.

This argument is valid, but is it sound? Is it really true that outing violates privacy? Defending this claim forces us to ask what the right to privacy protects and what it does not protect. Consequently, we need to develop a view of what privacy is, and why people have certain kinds of rights to privacy. Once these tasks are done we can show why outing is a violation of the right to privacy.

As you can see, our question and initial answer already require us to do a fair amount of work. However, more needs to be done if we are to convince those who may doubt that outing is immoral. We need to respond to a variety of objections and, in doing so, refine our position.

It might be objected, for example, that the outer reveals only a fact about a person's sexual orientation, and not any details of the outee's sex life, which clearly would be a violation of privacy. Moreover, publicly calling a person a heterosexual would <u>not</u> be an invasion of privacy, so why is publicizing a person's homosexuality a violation of their privacy? Answering this challenge begins with the observation that homosexuality is severely stigmatized in our society, while heterosexuality is not. Moreover, the right to privacy protects individuals from the indignity and humiliation of having the intimate parts of their lives held up to public scrutiny. No one blinks if you are revealed to be heterosexual, but you may well have a significant interest in not having someone reveal to possibly intolerant others that you are gay.

This argument still needs further development to be convincing, and there are other issues and considerations on both sides that would need to be examined. Perhaps outing is a violation of privacy in only *some* cases, but not in others. Such a distinction would have to be defended and justified. Finally, even if we agree that outing is a violation of privacy in a given case, it might be argued that the outing is *justified* because it will produce certain important benefits. Whether outing does produce such benefits, and whether it would be justified if it did, are questions that would also have to be answered.

My goal here has been to illustrate that the defense of any thesis requires constructing a whole framework of ideas, arranged in a logical order, with defense and refinement at every stage. When looked at philosophically, problems are almost never as simple as they might first appear. Solving a philosophical problem can therefore be a fairly complicated task. You cannot afford to procrastinate, thinking that you will be able to do a good job in a last minute effort. Plant the seed early: get the questions and issues into your head so that there will be sufficient time for them to germinate, grow, and flourish.

The only way to learn philosophical writing is by doing it. Write, subject your work to careful and objective criticism (your own and others'), and then re-write. Since it is often difficult to be objective about one's own work, it may be helpful to take a break from your work for a day or two and then come back to it with a fresh eye. Start early!

C. *The Introduction and Conclusion*

Any paper, on any topic, should have an introduction, body, and conclusion. However, the introduction (and conclusion) should probably be the last parts of the paper that you write. You obviously can't tell us what you are going to do until you know what that is. In short, you should have the position and arguments well-developed and refined before you even attempt the introduction. If you sit down to a blank page or screen and try to write your introduction without having done the bulk of the work, you are asking for a serious case of writer's block. Even if you are able to write an introduction you will probably find that it has to be thoroughly revised or even abandoned once you have written the body of the paper.

In the introduction, tell the reader where your essay is going by stating the thesis to be proved ("I will argue that..."). It will then be easier to see why you introduce your premises when you do. It is a surprising but provable fact that an infinite number of things follow from any given claim. Don't make your reader attempt to guess which of these consequences you're after by just tossing out your first premise. It is a very good idea to give a brief summary of the overall argument as soon as you have introduced the issue and stated your position. Give the reader a clear sense of the direction of the paper.

The concluding paragraph should restate or review your treatment of the issues, emphasizing the reasons you adopt the position you do. The conclusion should mirror your introduction. Make sure you have actually done what you said you were going to do in the paper. Your main goal in the conclusion is to remind the reader what you have accomplished, but you might also want to suggest how your research or argumentation has lead to other questions that warrant further exploration. This can impress on the reader that not only are you in full control of the issues you address in the paper, but that you are also aware of the place of your work in a broader philosophical context.

Chapter 6

Preparation of the Final Draft

A. *The Student as Author*

1. *Be Respectful*: Your attitude and tone should always be respectful; this is not an occasion to be snide, flippant, or crude. Both the subject matter and your reader deserve to be taken seriously. You are asking your grader to expend considerable time and energy in evaluating your effort to address a philosophical problem. If you do a slipshod job, you waste your own and your reader's time. A trivial, half-hearted, or sloppy effort is an insult to the reader and reflects badly on you.

2. *Be Truthful*: You should always try to ensure that what you say is true (or at least reasonable). You may not always succeed, but honest mistakes are honorable mistakes, and the possibility that you will say something false or open to challenge should not paralyze you. Write what you believe is true, and not what you think your instructor believes or wants to hear. This kind of second-guessing often rings untrue and is easily detected. Avoid trying to sound "deep" or sophisticated beyond your means. It is very difficult to *see* the truth of claims that are unclear or confusing.

3. *Express Your Beliefs*: In the past, students were often told to avoid speaking in the first person. Fortunately, this custom is weakening, and in philosophy there are good reasons to ignore it. You have been asked to write a paper on a philosophical problem; the grader wants to know what *you* think

after having wrestled with the issues. These are your ideas and you should be committed to them. Show the intellectual courage to take responsibility for them by filling your essay with such phrases as "I think that..." or "I will argue that...".

4. *Be Objective*: Stating your own beliefs does not mean that you are writing an autobiography or a confession. Your personal life and personal feelings *as such* are not relevant. How you *feel* about an issue has no pull at all on others; your feelings give others no reason to think the same way you do. Use "I argue" instead of "I feel". This implies that you have objective, and not merely subjective, grounds for your position. This means that you must support your claims with arguments. For *some* purposes you may draw on your personal experiences if they are representative of the human condition or are generalizable to many others (a still better strategy would be to pick a hypothetical "average person").

B. *Your Audience*

Your audience will most likely be your professor or teaching assistant, or both. Almost invariably the grader will know more about the subject than you do. He or she may also have a considered view of the topic, but do not attempt to "read their mind" and write what you think they want to hear. Intellectual dishonesty is easy to spot, and your argument will suffer if you are not really committed to it.

Your job is to show that you understand the issues with some thoroughness, have thought about them in detail, and have formed an opinion on the basis of carefully constructed arguments. Consequently, your writing should be both expository and persuasive—make your best case and defend it. A paper that does this will receive high marks even if it does not convince a grader to change his or her own view of the matter.

It may be better *not* to write strictly for your professor; this can lead one to assume too much, or assume that technical terms or doctrines do not need to be explained or defended. Remember, your job is to demonstrate that *you* know what you're talking about. Instead, I recommend that you assume your audience is intelligent but uninformed, and not necessarily philosophically sophisticated (e.g. your peers or your parents). It is far better to err on the side of caution. Defending or explaining something that is already accepted or understood by your audience is far better than assuming something that turns out to be and controversial.

Explain all technical terms in ordinary language, especially if you are using a term in a non-standard way. If necessary, give brief examples to make your meaning clear. Beware: many ordinary terms can take on technical meanings in philosophy. Granted, the grader probably already knows the meanings of most terms, but it is *your* knowledge that is at issue. It is your responsibility to show that you know the accepted usage of technical terms, or if you use a term in a novel way, to inform your reader of the idiosyncratic usage. In general, assume as little as possible (when in doubt, ask). Always use clear, straightforward language. Construct direct and simple sentences that say exactly what you mean. This will help to prevent confusion, vagueness, ambiguity and misunderstanding.

C. *Polishing*

After you have a draft the content of which is satisfactory, you should polish your prose. Here the emphasis is on ensuring that your grammar is correct and making some simple improvements in style.

If you write on a word processor use its spell-check program; it may also come with a grammar-check program. If your school has a writing center, take your draft to someone there and ask them to go over it with you. Ask a friend to read it. They don't have to be convinced, but they should at least be able to understand what you're trying to say. They can also help to spot typographical errors and other mistakes that you might have missed.

The importance of style is not that the prose be uniquely *yours* but that it communicate effectively. Here are some suggestions for improving style.

* avoid needless or uninformative qualification: "Descartes's position is not ~~actually~~ contradictory".
* reduce complex phrases: "Quine makes use of this distinction"—"Quine uses this distinction".
* use economical language: replace phrases with one word that means the same thing: "What people mean by 'human' can vary"—"The word 'human' is equivocal".
* transform passive verbs to active ("X was proved by Y" becomes "Y proved X").
* replace forms of the verb 'to be' with active verbs (replace "My argument will be..." with "I will argue that"...).

* avoid nominalization (changing verbs to nouns); e.g., use "She developed ..." instead of "The development of ...". By nominalizing verbs, one eliminates the agent doing the action, making the thought less clear.
* transform prepositional phrases with abstract nouns into clauses ("The reconstruction of Tooley's argument is difficult" becomes "Reconstructing Tooley's argument is difficult").
* use participial phrases to subordinate a thought expressed in a main clause: "Goldman attempted to develop a more plausible account of the value of sex. He rejected the means-end analyses of other philosophers."—"In developing a more plausible account of the value of sex, Goldman rejected the means-end analyses of other philosophers."
* make the antecedents of pronouns clear: "Americans are deeply divided over the morality of abortion. This is the topic of this essay." *What* is the topic? Abortion? The deep division of Americans' views? If the latter, then replace the second sentence with this: "This essay critically examines the main arguments for and against the morality of abortion."

These are only a few simple improvements in style that can be made. Consult any of the numerous books on composition for additional suggestions.

D. *Finishing Up*

It goes without saying that your paper should be typed. In this age of computers, you can eliminate the task of typing by using a word-processor. Composing on the computer can also significantly improve your writing because of the ease of editing and correcting. Number each page of text. Don't play with the margins or line-spacing in an attempt to "pad" a short paper (use one-inch margins all around, and double-space). These kinds of ploys are easy to spot and suggest to the reader that you are not willing to let what you have said stand on its own merits. Length by itself won't make or break your paper, though, of course, you should try to stay within the parameters set by your instructor. A well-written and carefully argued paper of a given length is definitely preferable to a somewhat longer paper of lesser quality.

When you've finished the final draft, run the Spell-checker one last time. Whether you use a word processor or not, *proofread carefully*! Don't undermine your efforts by making a bad impression. When you do the print-out, make sure it is readable, and double-check for printing errors.

For the convenience of the grader attach an extra blank page at the end so he or she can write comments. These can be invaluable in learning how to do better on future essays.

For your protection put your full name, your instructor's name, and the time and day of the class on the cover page. Put your last name or initials on all succeeding pages, then staple all the pages together. *Make a copy* for your records in case anything should happen to the copy you turn in; papers do sometimes get misplaced. It is also wise to keep a "hard" copy (photocopy) since copies on disk can be lost or damaged.

If you don't hand your paper directly to your instructor, have the person taking it note on it the time and date received. If you can, get a 'receipt' or, at least, get the person's name. Don't let a mishap undermine your hard work.

* *

Each of us is capable of thinking critically and carefully about philosophical questions. I hope the information and suggestions in this book help you in the writing of your paper, and reduce the level of anxiety that can be associated with such projects.

Happy Philosophizing!

* *

Bibliography

In addition to the *Encyclopedia of Philosophy* (cited below), the *Philosopher's Index* (published by the Philosophy Documentation Center), is a very helpful research resource. It catalogues philosophical articles appearing in scholarly journals, as well as anthologies and books. Ask your librarian for assistance; they may even have the *Philosopher's Index* 'on-line.'

Adler, Mortimer J. *Great Ideas from the Great Books*. New York: Washington Square Press, 1961.

Bontempo, Charles J., and S. Jack Odell, eds. *The Owl of Minerva: Philosophers on Philosophy*. New York: McGraw Hill, 1975.

Chicago Manual of Style. 13th ed. Chicago: University of Chicago Press, 1982.

Cornman, Lehrer, and Pappas. *Philosophical Problems and Arguments: An Introduction*. New York: Macmillan, 1982.

Durant, Will. *The Story of Philosophy*. New York: Pocket Books, 1957.

Edwards, Paul, ed. *The Encyclopedia of Philosophy*. New York: Macmillan & Free Press, 1967.

Honer, Stanley and Hunt, Thomas, *Invitation to Philosophy: Issues and Options* (4th ed) Belmont CA.: Wadsworth Publishing Co., 1982.

Johnson, A. H. *Philosophers in Action*. Columbus, Ohio: Charles E. Merrill, 1977.

Kahane, Howard. Logic and Philosophy. Belmont, CA: Wadsworth, 1984.

Martinich, A. P. *Philosophical Writing, An Introduction.* Englewood Cliffs, N.J.: Prentice Hall, 1989.

Michalos, Alex C. *Improving Your Reasoning.* Englewood Cliffs, N.J.: Prentice-Hall, 1970.

Moore and Parker, *Critical Thinking* (2nd ed) Mountain View, Ca.: Mayfield Publishing Co., 1989.

Rosenberg, Jay F. *The Practice of Philosophy: A Handbook for Beginners.* Prentice-Hall, Englewood Cliffs, N.J., 1978.

Russell, Bertrand. *The Problems of Philosophy.* New York: Oxford University Press (Galaxy Book), 1959.

Salmon, Wesley. Logic. 2nd ed. Englewood Cliffs, NJ: Prentice Hall, 1981.

Scriven, Michael. *Reasoning.* New York: McGraw-Hill, 1976.

Seech, Zachary. *Writing Philosophy Papers.* Belmont, CA: Wadsworth, 1993.

Sprague, Elmer. *What is Philosophy: A Short Introduction.* New York: Oxford University Press, 1961.

Strunk and White. *Elements of Style.* 3rd ed. New York: Macmillan, 1979.

Vivian, Frederick. *Thinking Philosophically: An Introduction for Students.* New York: Basic Books, Inc., 1969.

Index